Gino's

ITALIAN ESCAPE

A TASTE OF THE SUN

Gino's

ITALIAN ESCAPE

A TASTE OF THE SUN

HODDER &
STOUGHTON

GINO D'ACAMPO

I want to dedicate this book to my beautiful children, Luciano, Rocco and Mia, for continuing to give me the strength and unconditional love that helps me through tough days.

INTRODUCTION / 8

Antipasti & aperitivi
ANTIPASTI E APERITIVI / 12

Soups
ZUPPE / 40

Stews & bakes
STUFATI E PIATTI AL FORNO / 58

Fish & seafood
PESCE E FRUTTI DI MARE / 80

Pasta
PASTA / 104

Rice & risotto
RISO E RISOTTI / 130

Meat & game
CARNE E SELVAGGINA / 152

Pizza & bread
PIZZA E PANE / 178

Sides & salads
CONTORNI E INSALATE / 194

Desserts
DOLCE / 216

INDEX / 250

After the huge success of *Gino's Italian Escape* I was so excited to be asked again to revisit more of my beautiful home country. This time I delved into the northern regions of Italy (although I say that loosely as some regions, such as Tuscany, are technically in central Italy!), where less familiar but just as wonderful cities and foods awaited me: Venice, Burano, Bologna, Modena, Parma, Florence, Siena, Genoa – all are amazing places to visit and I got to enjoy each and every one on a fabulous three-week journey.

I often get asked what I think the main differences are between the north and the south of Italy and my answer would always be quite vague, as I truly believe that sometimes there are such vast differences that it is like being in different

countries, rather than just regions. The north of Italy has been influenced more by the Germans and Celts who happen to inhabit neighbouring countries, while the south of Italy has been largely influenced by the Greeks. Economy-wise the two parts of the country have stark differences: the north is industrialised – the three corners of the industrial triangle (Milan, Turin and Genoa) have become the wealthiest regions in the whole country – while the south still remains more of a rural region with a warmer climate and a more natural agriculture.

The divide does not end there, as the inhabitants of both parts of the country consider themselves to have very different personalities – some southerners believe the northerners to be cold

INTRODUCTION

and money-orientated while some northerners might argue that the southerners are the lower class of the country.

I personally think that today, most Italians would say that the main difference between the two areas is apparent in the food they serve. Because northern Italy is historically a much wealthier region, their cuisine is more affiliated with richer dishes – they use a lot of butter and cream – whereas those in the south grow olives in the warmer climate which they press for oil and live off the fresh vegetables they produce.

Meat is most popular amongst the northern Italians, who use a lot of it in their cooking; they keep excellent cattle and hog breeds and as a result beef, veal and pork are the meats of choice, with lamb playing a lesser role. The way meat is prepared ranges from frying to stewing and boiling, and it is often cooked in wine or broth flavoured with chopped herbs. Northern Italians also include a lot of rice and polenta in their meals, and in the winter they create rich hearty soups, while the southern Italians tend to use tomato-based sauces and eat cured meats and pulses – and because they have a larger coastline than their northern neighbours, fish is definitely more popular than meat. Whichever region you are from, though, the Italian people are some of the healthiest in the world – so both areas must be doing something right!

INTRODUCTION

Cheese is a large part of all regional cuisines in Italy and the most commonly known – Parmesan, mozzarella, ricotta and Gorgonzola – only scratch the surface of Italian dairy. Because Italy makes cheeses using cow, goat, buffalo and sheep milks, the range of varieties and flavours is immense, with each region offering its own specialities and spins on the classics. If I had to choose three of my favourites from this part of Italy I would choose Marzolino del Chianti, a young soft cheese made with raw ewe's milk in the Chianti region which has an intense flavour; Brillo di Treviso, a red-wine-washed soft, pasteurised cow's milk cheese from Venice which has a fruity flavour of Italian red wine and can be easily melted – so it's great for cooking; and, of course, the famous Parmigiano Reggiano, which is produced within the provinces of Parma, Reggio Emilia, Modena and Bologna. Italian law is very strict and the true Parmigiano Reggiano – a popular cow's milk cheese that boasts up to 36 months of ageing, can only be sold as such if it is produced in these areas.

One thing the north and south definitely have in common is their love for pasta. Today, both areas use all kinds of pasta in their cooking, but they will still each have different versions of the accompanying sauces. A very popular option in the north of Italy is egg pasta, which has a richer colour and flavour, and a regional favourite is farfalle, the bow-shaped pasta, which originated in Emilia-Romagna and Lombardy and is used for lighter creamier sauces. Tortellini is also much enjoyed in the north, and while in Bologna I got a chance to make the real thing!

Another passion all Italians share – wherever they are from – is good wine. Italy offers a larger, more diverse array of wine styles than almost any other nation, so this paragraph had the potential to be huge. So instead I decided to mention here just three of my favourites from the north of Italy: Pinot Grigio – typically a light-bodied, crisp, fresh white wine which originates from Venice; Chianti – a dry red wine made from the Sangiovese grape in a blend that is hugely popular worldwide; and finally the very special Brunello di Montalcino. This wine is one of the more expensive in the region and is produced from a blend of grapes to create a complex flavour which ages very well. It is often drunk with meats and game, so it is a very popular choice when dining out. Of course, in the north wine is not only used for drinking but is also nearly always used in cooking too, so its production plays an important part in the lives of northern Italians!

I hope this introduction to the beautiful and fascinating north of Italy has whetted your appetite and intrigued you enough that you want to read on and try some of my new recipes that I have discovered or created on my journey. I hope that in making them you enjoy the flavours that my wonderful trip brought me and experience a taste of the real Italy. As always, my dishes are easy to create, I will never let you down and still stand strong in saying …

Minimum Effort, Maximum Satisfaction!

Enjoy, and *Buon appetito!*

ANTIPASTI & APERITIVI

I don't think I've ever had a meal in Italy without having some kind of antipasti first, even when I'm eating informally in someone's home. Unlike most other nationalities, we Italians never serve just one plate of food for a main meal at lunch or dinner – especially if we are cooking for all the family. Antipasti of some kind will always be on offer – whether it's a full-blown selection or just a simple plate of grilled vegetables, regional cheeses or cured meats and salami – with, of course, that must-have ingredient: warm rustic bread. To Italians, antipasti without bread is like fish without chips – it just doesn't feel right. That attitude is not peculiar to the northern regions either, the southern Italians are just as particular about it!

In northern Italy antipasti are very much put into two sections on a menu. You will probably find that they are divided into land or sea starters, rather than the traditional hot or cold. The most common antipasti are predominantly cold dishes ranging from a wonderful selection of cured meats, which are particularly fabulous in Bologna and Parma. Grilled vegetables also feature, which will be what is in season in the local area – in Pisa and Florence these are eaten in abundance. Local cheeses will also have their place, including regional specialities such as Gorgonzola, Taleggio, Parmigiano-Reggiano, and of course no antipasti course is complete without octopus salad and fresh anchovies. You will also find some amazing hot or warm regional specialities on offer, such as

14

arancini (rice balls), crispy fried polenta and warm *caponata* (aubergine and vegetable ratatouille). What I love most about antipasti, though, is the presentation of all the different elements and the colours and smells that just get your taste buds flowing.

The most important thing about this course is the care and time taken to plate the food; it reminds you and your guests that mealtimes are for relaxing, pleasure and indulgence, as well as opportunities to do a simple 'how was your day?'. We often forget to do this in our busy lives, and yet it is so important to Italian families and, I would argue, any family. So if nothing else, prepare a few of these dishes for your family, tuck in and enjoy being together with good food. It's definitely the best part of my day.

Three cicchetti / TRE CICCHETTI

Cicchetti are little bar snacks that are unique to Venice, so it is the perfect place to try them – you can even have a tour of the bars that serve these little plates of deliciousness! In Venice these dishes often feature seafood, but there are other options too. Cicchetti are always best served with a glass of chilled Italian white wine.

Serves 4

12 thin slices of ciabatta, griddled or toasted

For the courgette cicchetti
1 courgette, cut into very fine matchsticks
1 tablespoon chopped fresh chives
¼ fennel bulb, finely sliced
1 tablespoon small capers
1 tablespoon extra virgin olive oil
Salt and ground white pepper to taste

For the two mayonnaises
4 tablespoons mayonnaise
1 tablespoon medium chilli powder
Peeled and finely diced rind of ½ lemon, plus
   a little juice

For the crispy cod cicchetti
100g skinless cod fillet
3 tablespoons toasted fine breadcrumbs
2 tablespoons mild chilli powder
1 egg
4 tablespoons olive oil
Sea salt flakes

For the prawn cicchetti
6 large prawns, peeled

1. Make the courgette cicchetti by putting the courgette, chives, fennel and capers in a bowl. Season with salt and pepper then add the extra virgin olive oil. Mix well and set aside for 10 minutes.

2. Make the two lots of mayonnaise by mixing 2 tablespoons of mayonnaise with the chilli powder in one bowl, then in another bowl mix the remaining mayonnaise with the lemon rind and juice. Set both to one side.

3. Cut the cod on a slight angle into really thin slices. Combine the breadcrumbs and chilli powder on one plate and beat the egg on another plate. Dip the cod slices into the egg, then shake off any excess and roll in the breadcrumb mix, pressing down to evenly cover.

4. Heat the olive oil in a frying pan and fry the cod for 1 minute. Turn and cook for another minute only. Add the prawns and cook for 15 seconds. Remove the cod and prawns from the pan and transfer to a plate lined with kitchen paper to drain.

5. Take four pieces of toast and top each with a little of the lemon mayo. Take four more and top with the chilli mayo. Slice the prawns into rings and place them, in a line, on top of the chilli-mayo toasts. Cut each piece of breaded cod in half and place on top of the lemon-mayo toasts, then sprinkle over the sea salt flakes. Finally, top the last four toasts with the courgette and fennel salad. Serve all the toasts together on a big platter for everyone to help themselves, or divide among 4 little side plates for individual bites.

Chicken liver pâté with Marsala wine / PATE DI FEGATO E MARSALA

There are so many pâtés available in the supermarkets but none have the same beautiful fresh flavour as one that is home-made. Although Marsala is produced in Sicily, it is a wine that is popular throughout the country in cooking, and in the north it is served as a drink to accompany local cheeses. For a more intense orange flavour and less of an alcoholic kick, you could replace the Cognac with the zest of the clementine.

Serves 4

2 tablespoons olive oil
400g chicken livers
1 small onion, peeled and chopped
1 tablespoon fresh thyme leaves
3 tablespoons Marsala wine
100g salted butter, plus 40g butter, melted
Juice of 1 clementine
1 tablespoon Cognac
Salt and ground white pepper to taste

1. Heat 1 tablespoon of oil in a medium-sized frying pan over a medium heat and fry the chicken livers for 10 minutes, stirring frequently with a wooden spoon. Remove with a slotted spoon and transfer to a food processor or blender.

2. In the same pan, add the remaining olive oil and gently fry the onion and thyme for about 3 minutes. Pour in the Marsala wine and let it bubble for 30 seconds, scraping up all the lovely brown caramelised bits from the bottom of the pan using a wooden spoon – that is where all the flavour is.

3. Tip the onion mixture, with all the pan juices, into the food processor and add in the 100g butter, clementine juice and Cognac. Season with salt and pepper then whizz to a smooth paste.

4. Spoon the mixture into ramekins or one larger dish and pour over the 40g of melted butter. Leave the pâté to set in the fridge, covered with cling film, for 3 hours.

5. Serve with warm crusty bread and perhaps a cold glass of Italian white wine.

Gorgonzola, fig and prosciutto wraps / ROTOLINI DI PROSCIUTTO CON FICHI E GORGONZOLA

Salty prosciutto together with the sweetness of the figs is always a winner for me. Creamy Gorgonzola works well here, or you could use another northern Italian favourite: Taleggio. This is the quickest recipe ever – even my kids only need 10 minutes to prepare this! Enjoy as a snack, or bring them along on your picnic.

1. Preheat the grill to medium. Place the figs on a baking tray and using a sharp knife, cut a cross three-quarters of the way down into each. Divide the Gorgonzola into 8 pieces and stuff one piece into each cross. Wrap each fig in a slice of Parma ham and drizzle over a little chilli oil. Place under the grill for 5 minutes until the ham is beginning to crisp.

Serves 4

8 large ripe figs
100g Gorgonzola cheese
8 slices of Parma ham
4 tablespoons chilli oil
120g rocket leaves
Balsamic glaze for drizzling

2. Meanwhile, divide the rocket leaves among four serving plates and set aside.

3. Place two wrapped figs onto each serving plate and spoon over the oil that's spilled out from the sides of the figs while cooking. Drizzle over a little balsamic glaze and serve with a few slices of ciabatta bread. *Buon appetito!*

21

Prawn skewers with lemon, butter and chilli / SPIEDINI DI GAMBERONI CON LIMONE, BURRO E PEPERONCINO

Prawns are so delicious as well as being a good source of protein and low in calories. This recipe is very simple; threading the prawns onto skewers makes it much easier to turn them over while they are cooking under the grill. You can make this dish as part of a lunch or dinner with friends – I promise they'll love you forever!

Serves 4

500g raw peeled king prawns
50g salted butter, softened
Grated zest and juice of 1 large unwaxed lemon
2 red chillies, deseeded and finely chopped
Salt to taste
Handful of chopped fresh flat leaf parsley
  to serve

1. Preheat the grill to high. Thread the prawns onto small metal skewers and lay on a baking tray. (If you use wooden skewers, soak them in water for 20 minutes beforehand, otherwise they will burn.)

2. Cream the butter with the lemon zest and chillies and season. Brush the butter over the prawns. Transfer the skewers and the baking tray to the grill and cook for 5 minutes or until the prawns have turned pink, turning them over halfway through the cooking time.

3. Remove from the grill, pour the lemon juice over the prawns and shake the tray to mix the sauce together.

4. Lay the skewers on a large serving dish and pour over the spicy lemon-butter sauce then sprinkle over the chopped parsley. Serve with a green salad and thick chunks of bread to mop up the juices.

Aubergine, tomato and mozzarella stack / TORRE DI MELANZANE, POMODORI E MOZZARELLA

This is a simple version of the classic northern Italian baked dish, *melanzane alla parmigiana*. Perfect as antipasti or a light lunch with crusty bread, these elegant little stacks contain all the fresh flavours of Italy – aubergine, juicy tomatoes, creamy mozzarella, salty Parmesan and basil-infused olive oil. *Delizioso!*

Serves 4 (starters / light lunch)

10g fresh basil leaves, finely chopped
50ml extra virgin olive oil
Salt and ground black pepper to taste
2 tablespoons olive oil
1 large aubergine, cut into 8 x 1cm thick discs
2 large beef tomatoes, tops and bottoms removed and each cut into 4 rounds
A few Parmesan cheese shavings
2 balls of mozzarella, each cut into 4 rounds

1. Put the chopped basil in a small bowl, pour over the extra virgin olive oil, season with salt and pepper and set aside to infuse.

2. Heat a large frying pan over a high heat and add the olive oil. Add the aubergine to the pan, season with salt and pepper and cook for 90 seconds on each side or until the slices are golden brown and tender. Remove from the pan and transfer to a tray in a warm place. Add the tomatoes to the pan and cook for 30 seconds on each side, then remove from the heat and season with salt and pepper.

3. Place a disc of aubergine in the middle of each plate and top with some Parmesan shavings, then a tomato disc and then a mozzarella round. Repeat this pattern to finish with a slice of mozzarella. Once all four stacks are complete, drizzle over some of the basil-infused olive oil and serve.

Sardines with basil and lemon butter / SARDINE CON BURRO AL BASILICO E LIMONE

Sardines or young pilchards are eaten in most of the Mediterranean countries and are almost a staple of all the coastal areas around Italy. This is my good friend Darren's favourite fish dish. I made this when he came over recently and he demolished so many of the sardines that I thought he might swim home!

Serves 6

12 large sardines (about 80–100g each)
Olive oil for brushing
Salt and freshly ground black pepper to taste
60g salted butter
25g fresh basil leaves, roughly chopped
Juice and zest of 1 unwaxed lemon
1 shallot, peeled and finely chopped

1. Preheat the grill to high. First prepare the sardines. Remove the scales with the back of a kitchen knife. Cut the stomachs open and scrape out the contents (particularly any dark blood) and discard. Give the fish a good wash, inside and out, under cold water and pat dry with kitchen paper. Brush the sardines with olive oil and season with salt and pepper inside and out before laying them flat on a baking tray. Set aside.

2. In a small saucepan, melt the butter for 2 minutes on a medium heat with the basil, juice and zest of the lemon and the chopped shallot. Season with salt and pepper. Drizzle the butter over the sardines on the tray and place under the hot grill for 5 minutes, then turn them over to cook on the other side for 5 minutes more, until cooked through.

3. Transfer the sardines to a large, warmed platter and pour over the buttery juices from the bottom of the baking tray. Serve immediately with any salad of your choice.

Smoked trout with artichokes and cannellini beans / TROTA
AFFUMICATA CON CARCIOFI E CANNELLINI

Whilst completely delicious, this recipe calls for raw onion in the salad and raw garlic in the dressing, so can I suggest that you and your partner make a pact to eat it together? Like all Italian food, this dish tastes even better when you have someone to share it with!

Serves 4

1 x 400g tin cannellini beans, drained and rinsed
1 small red onion, peeled and finely sliced
60g pitted green olives in brine, drained and
    cut in half
150g chargrilled artichoke hearts in oil, drained
    and roughly sliced
6 tablespoons extra virgin olive oil
2 lemons (juice and zest of 1 lemon, 1 cut into
    wedges)
4 tablespoons chopped fresh flat leaf parsley
1 garlic clove, peeled and crushed
Salt and freshly ground black pepper to taste
150g smoked trout fillets

1. TIp the beans into a medium-sized bowl and add the onion, olives and artichokes. Set aside.

2. In a small bowl, whisk together the olive oil with the juice and zest of 1 lemon, the parsley and garlic. Season with salt and pepper.

3. Pour half of the dressing over the beans mixture and mix well. Transfer to a large serving plate and scatter over the trout, breaking it into pieces as you do so. Pour over the remaining dressing and serve garnished with the lemon wedges.

Griddled courgette salad with chilli dressing / INSALATA DI ZUCCHINE GRIGLIATE

Parmesan is a real taste of northern Italy, specifically its home in Emilia-Romagna. Many people think that Parmesan cheese should be reserved only for sprinkling over pasta. I urge you to try it in a salad or in other dishes as a main ingredient. Don't buy the ready-grated cheese – it is always far better and more delicious if you buy a good piece and grate it yourself.

Serves 6

6 courgettes, washed and thinly sliced
  lengthways
Olive oil for brushing
50g shelled pistachio nuts, lightly crushed
25g fresh basil leaves, roughly chopped
150g Parmesan cheese, roughly chopped into
  little pieces
Salt and freshly ground black pepper to taste
Balsamic glaze for drizzling

For the dressing
6 tablespoons extra virgin olive oil
Juice of 2 lemons
1 teaspoon runny honey
2 red chillies, deseeded and finely chopped

1. Heat a griddle pan over a high heat. Brush the courgette slices with the olive oil and cook in batches on the griddle pan for about 2 minutes on each side or until they are charred. Transfer the courgettes to a big bowl and add in the pistachios, basil and Parmesan. Season with salt and pepper and toss everything together.

2. Combine all the ingredients for the dressing in a small bowl and pour over the courgette salad, making sure the slices are all coated.

3. Arrange the salad on a large serving plate and finish with a drizzle of balsamic glaze all over.

Red peppers stuffed with Taleggio / PEPERONI RIPIENI DI TALEGGIO

The pepper... so Mediterranean, but in fact it is originally from South America. This vegetable was introduced to Italy towards the end of the eighteenth century and has now become an integral part of Italian cuisine. I love this recipe because it is very simple to prepare and very colourful to serve.

Serves 6

3 large red peppers, halved and deseeded
1 tablespoon olive oil
200g Taleggio cheese, cut into 12 slices
   each ½cm thick

For the dressing
Juice of 1 lemon
1 garlic clove, peeled and crushed
1 red chilli, deseeded and finely chopped
40g shelled walnuts, roughly chopped
3 tablespoons chopped fresh flat leaf parsley
3 tablespoons extra virgin olive oil
Balsamic glaze for drizzling

1. Heat a large frying pan over a high heat. Brush the pepper halves with the olive oil and cook in the pan, cut side down, for 5 minutes, until beginning to soften. Turn the peppers over and place 2 slices of Taleggio in each half. Leave to cook for a further 8 minutes or until the cheese has melted and the peppers have softened. Pop under a hot preheated grill for 2 minutes to brown the cheese.

32

2. Meanwhile, prepare the dressing. In a small bowl, combine the lemon juice, garlic, chilli, walnuts, parsley and extra virgin olive oil. Whisk until combined.

3. Arrange the peppers on a large serving platter and drizzle over the dressing. Add a final zigzag drizzle of balsamic glaze over the peppers and serve immediately with warm crusty bread.

Courgette and ricotta tart /

TORTA SALATA DI ZUCCHINE E RICOTTA

This is the perfect tart to serve as an antipasto or as part of a buffet. I've made it several times for friends and there's always a fight over the last piece.

Serves 6

320g pack ready-rolled puff pastry
1 tablespoon olive oil
2 courgettes, thinly sliced
250g ricotta cheese
2 eggs, beaten
2 tablespoons sun-dried tomato purée
Handful of chopped fresh basil
Pinch of grated nutmeg
1 tablespoon freshly grated Parmesan cheese
2 tablespoons balsamic glaze

1. Preheat the oven to 180°C/gas mark 4. Take the puff pastry out of the fridge to bring to room temperature while you prepare the other ingredients.

2. Put the olive oil in a large frying pan over a medium heat and fry the courgettes for 10 minutes or until they are golden around the edges. Remove with a slotted spoon and set aside.

3. In a medium bowl, mix the ricotta, eggs, sun-dried tomato purée, basil, nutmeg and Parmesan.

4. Line a baking tray with baking parchment, unroll the pastry and lay it on the paper. Spread the ricotta mixture over the pastry leaving a 1cm border around the edge. Place the courgettes on top of the ricotta, overlapping the slices in rows. Pinch the pastry base at the corners to raise the edges and make a frame so the ricotta doesn't seep out during cooking.

5. Cook in the oven for 30 minutes until the pastry turns a golden brown. Leave to cool slightly then drizzle with balsamic glaze before cutting into 6 slices and serving.

Grissini wrapped in Parma ham with creamy pesto dip / INVOLTINI DI GRISSINI E PROSCIUTTO

Is it any wonder that basil takes such a central position in Italian cuisine? Could it be perhaps because it has the most incredible flavour? This fragrant herb can transform dishes from average to special in seconds, just so long as the basil is fresh and not dried. For this recipe you only need a small amount of fresh basil pesto, but the ingredients listed here will make more than you need because it's fantastic to have some in the fridge for that moment when you're too lazy to cook. Stir it through some hot pasta and there you have it – two meals for the price of one!

Serves 4

8 grissini sticks
16 slices of Parma ham

For the pesto dip
50g toasted pine nuts
100g fresh basil leaves
50g freshly grated Parmesan cheese
150ml extra virgin olive oil, plus extra
  for drizzling
2 garlic cloves, peeled and chopped
Salt and freshly ground black pepper
200g mascarpone cheese

1. To prepare the pesto dip, put the pine nuts, basil, Parmesan, oil and garlic in a food processor or blender and blitz until smooth. Season with salt and black pepper. Whizz again for a few seconds. Alternatively, grind to a smooth paste in a pestle and mortar. Mix the mascarpone with 2½ tablespoons of the basil pesto and transfer to a serving bowl. Drizzle over a little extra virgin olive oil.

2. Break each grissini into two. Wrap a slice of prosciutto around each one, leaving a centimetre uncovered at one end so the grissini can be held easily. Serve the grissini with the dip and enjoy the party.

Aperol Spritz / APERITIVO VENEZIANO
ALL'APEROL

The Italian Spritz is a refreshing drink that is commonly served in the northern part of Italy, especially Venice, which gives it its other name – Spritz Veneziano. Many Venetian towns have their own version of this drink, and in the last decade, the Aperol Spritz has become extremely popular across Italy, made with Prosecco and Aperol, an Italian orange liqueur. Aperol Spritz is one of the lightest alcoholic cocktails, so as far as I'm concerned that's a green light to enjoy it!

serves 4

Ice cubes
400ml Prosecco
275ml Aperol
125ml soda water
Orange slices to garnish

1. Fill four highball or wine glasses one-quarter full with ice.

2. In a large jug, pour in the Prosecco, then the Aperol. Add in the soda water and stir gently with a wooden spoon.

3. Pour into the glasses and garnish each with one or two orange slices. *Salute!*

SOUPS

Why is it that the aroma of soups seems to bring back a mood or memory, giving you the feeling of warmth and being taken care of? Perhaps it's the time and love it takes to create. For years it was the basic diet for all children in Italy; parents knew it was an extremely healthy and filling meal, as well as inexpensive. Personally, I see myself doing it with my own children, I think it's one of the first culinary options we offer if anyone feels ill or sad.

While on my journey around the north of Italy, I got to sample some great varieties of soups, from the typical meat-filled pasta in a clear broth to the amazing chunky sausage, pea and bread combination we ate in Florence.

Traditionally, soups are classified into two categories: clear broths and thick soups. Every town in Italy will make a completely different version of a similar dish and many locals say 'Tell me what soup you prefer and I'll tell you where you come from'. In Italy, cooking traditions define people's identities, not just their dialects.

The lighter broth options are normally served as a starter in Italy, while the thicker, more rustic options are a meal in themselves. Rice – such as the ever-present carnaroli – breads, pulses and pasta are firm favourites in all the thicker northern recipes. Light broths and fish soups are predominantly served hot in Italy, but many of the other variations are often enjoyed warm or even cold. Unlike most countries, in Italy soups tend to be eaten all year round, even in the height of summer.

One thing that all Italian soups have in common, though, regardless of the region they originate from, is that they all consist of a good broth. Many people take hours, even days, to create the perfect broth, but most of us nowadays use the recipe ingredients to make a natural broth that is slightly enhanced by herbs and stock. Either way, soups are incredibly healthy and good for you, so I hope you enjoy my selection. Be as creative as you wish – anything goes.

Culatello, onion and bean soup /

ZUPPA DI CULATELLO, CIPOLLE E FAGIOLI

In Italy we've used onions for thousands of years; they were introduced to the country by the Egyptians, but were quickly taken up by the Romans. Larger onions are better for cooking, the smaller ones for salads and pickles. Whichever you use, when you cut into them they release an enzyme that reacts with the rest of the onion to release a gas. When that gas combines with water, it creates an acid, and if that gets in your eye, it will sting. The best way to avoid crying over chopped onions is to breathe through your mouth and stick your tongue out as you chop – this draws the gas over your wet tongue before it gets to your tear ducts. You may look odd but it'll stop the tears flowing. Alternatively, get someone else to chop the onions for you! Culatello is the best Italian cold cut of prosciutto you can buy, with a flavour that beats all other hams. If you can't get this, though, just use a good pancetta.

Serves 4

25g salted butter
1 tablespoon olive oil
150g diced Culatello or pancetta
500g large white onions, peeled and finely sliced
2 teaspoons caster sugar
15g plain flour
2 tablespoons red wine
1 litre hot beef stock, made with stock cubes
1 x 400g tin borlotti beans, drained
Salt and freshly ground black pepper
4 tablespoons freshly grated Parmesan cheese

1. Melt the butter with the oil in a medium saucepan. Add in the Culatello and gently fry for 5 minutes until browned, stirring occasionally with a wooden spoon. Remove the Culatello with a slotted spoon and set aside.

2. Add the onions to the pan and fry for 3 minutes, stirring frequently, until they start to soften. Add the caster sugar and continue to cook over a low heat, stirring occasionally, for 20 minutes until the onions have caramelised. Sprinkle the flour over the onions and cook for a further 2 minutes, stirring continuously.

3. Gradually stir in the wine and the stock. Add the Culatello and borlotti beans and season with salt and pepper. Simmer for 30 minutes, stirring occasionally.

4. Serve immediately, sprinkled with the Parmesan.

Traditional north Italian chicken soup / BRODO DI POLLO CLASSICO

The ultimate feel-better recipe. One bowl of this and the world is a brighter place. This recipe always tastes better if you cook it one day before you need it. Once it is cool, cover it with cling film so that the sheet is clinging to the top of the soup. Put it in the fridge and the fat will rise to the top and cling to the film, then when it is completely cold, swiftly remove the cling film and all the fat will be removed too, leaving a relatively fat-free, non-greasy, healthy soup.

Serves 10

1 whole chicken (about 1.8kg)
1 leek
4 celery sticks
1 tablespoon salt
½ teaspoon ground white pepper
2 large carrots, peeled and cut into 4cm pieces
2 turnips, peeled
2 chicken stock cubes
5 tablespoons freshly grated Parmesan cheese
20 small fresh basil leaves
Slices of toasted ciabatta to serve

1. Place the chicken into a large saucepan. Pour in 3.5 litres of cold water and bring to the boil, skimming and discarding any foam that rises to the top.

2. Tie the leek and celery sticks together with cooking string and add to the chicken along with the salt, white pepper, carrots and turnips. Crumble in the stock cubes, bring to the boil and leave to simmer for 3 hours, uncovered.

3. Remove the turnips, squeeze on a slotted spoon over the saucepan to release all their liquid and discard. Remove and discard the tied celery and leeks. Remove the chicken, place on a chopping board and discard the bones and skin.

4. Shred the chicken meat and return it to the soup. Heat through and serve hot scattered with a little Parmesan, a few basil leaves and some slices of toasted ciabatta.

Beef and cannellini bean soup /

BRODO ALLA FRIULIANA

Pearl barley is often used in soups in Italy, especially in the Alto Adige and Friuli regions in the north. You won't need much else to eat after a large bowl of this, because it is a very hearty soup – my idea of a hug in bowl. You can replace the cannellini beans with borlotti beans if you prefer.

1. Heat the oil in a large saucepan and fry the onion, carrot and celery over a gentle heat for 5 minutes, until softened but not browned. Stir occasionally with a wooden spoon.

Serves 4

1 tablespoon olive oil
1 large onion, peeled and grated
1 carrot, peeled and finely chopped
1 celery stick, finely chopped
75g pearl barley
1 litre hot beef stock, made with stock cubes
500g boneless beef shin, roughly chopped
3 rib bones (or about 1kg of beef bones – ask
   your butcher)
1 x 400g tin cannellini beans, drained
500g passata (sieved tomatoes)
Salt and freshly ground black pepper
3 tablespoons chopped fresh flat leaf parsley

2. Place the pearl barley in a sieve and give it a good rinse under cold water. Add the barley to the pan together with the stock, meat, bones, cannellini beans and passata. Season with salt and pepper. Slowly bring to the boil then simmer for 2 hours with the lid on.

3. Remove and discard the bones. Chop the beef into bite-sized pieces and ladle into soup bowls. Scatter over some freshly chopped parsley and serve immediately with plenty of crusty bread.

Smooth fennel and tomato soup with prawns / VELLUTATA DI FINOCCHI E POMODORI CON GAMBERI

This is a great soup to eat if you are on a diet. No butter, no milk or cream, just maximum taste from the fresh fennel and dill. If you prefer your soup to be a little thinner, add a little more passata. You could also replace the prawns with cooked mussels if you prefer.

Serves 6

2 tablespoons olive oil
1 large onion, peeled and sliced
2 large fennel bulbs, halved, cores removed and sliced
1 medium potato, peeled and cut into quarters
800ml hot vegetable stock, made with stock cubes
500ml passata (sieved tomatoes)
1 bay leaf
200g cooked peeled prawns
1 tablespoon chopped fresh dill, plus extra to garnish
Salt and black pepper to taste

1. Heat the oil in a large saucepan and fry the onion over a medium heat for 8 minutes until starting to soften. Stir occasionally with a wooden spoon. Add the fennel to the onions and fry for 2 minutes. Add the potato, vegetable stock, passata and bay leaf. Bring to the boil, cover the pan with a lid and simmer for 25 minutes.

2. Take the pan off the heat and remove and discard the bay leaf. Blitz the soup with a hand blender until smooth. Add in the prawns, reserving a few for a garnish, with the chopped dill and continue to simmer for a further 10 minutes. Season to taste.

3. Serve hot sprinkled with the reserved prawns and garnished with a little dill.

White fish soup with melted Taleggio toasts / ZUPPA DI PESCE CON CROSTINI E TALEGGIO FUSO

Looking at this list of ingredients you'd be forgiven for thinking that this soup would be too heavy and difficult to prepare, but I promise you it's surprisingly light and simple. I use a combination of halibut, haddock and cod but you could also use monkfish, sea bass or even some prawns. Taleggio is one of Italy's best-loved cheeses, and although I don't often use cheese with fish, this combination is perfect.

1. Heat the oil in a large saucepan and add in the leeks, celery, potato, carrot and red pepper. Cook gently, stirring occasionally, for 10 minutes or until the vegetables start to soften. Tip in the chopped tomatoes and fish and cook for 5 minutes, stirring occasionally. Pour in the stock, white wine, basil and parsley and bring to the boil. Season with salt and pepper and simmer for 40 minutes.

Serves 6

4 tablespoons olive oil
2 leeks, roughly chopped
1 celery stick, roughly chopped
1 potato, peeled and roughly chopped
1 carrot, peeled and roughly chopped
½ red pepper, deseeded and roughly chopped
1 x 400g tin chopped tomatoes
500g mixed white fish, skin removed and
  roughly chopped
1 litre hot fish stock, made with stock cubes
250ml Italian dry white wine
Handful of fresh basil leaves
Handful of fresh flat leaf parsley
Salt and white pepper to taste
100ml double cream
6 small slices of day-old bread
6 small slices of Taleggio cheese, rind removed

2. Remove from the heat and blitz until smooth with a hand blender. Pour in the cream and return to the heat. Leave to simmer while you prepare the cheese on toast.

3. Heat the grill and place the bread under it until brown on one side. Turn the bread over and place a slice of Taleggio on each piece. Grill again until the cheese starts to melt.

4. Ladle the soup into serving bowls and float a Taleggio toast in each bowl. Serve immediately with a large glass of cold Italian white wine.

Spinach and lemon soup / VELLUTATA
DI SPINACI E LIMONE

Spinach is grown in northern and central Italy where the climate is mild but not too hot. Available all year round, spinach is packed with iron and contains large amounts of vitamins A and C. The reason for not adding all the spinach to this recipe at once during cooking is that if you add half just before blending the soup, you end up with the most vibrant of colours. This is a soup Popeye would be proud of!

Serves 4

50g salted butter
1 onion, peeled and roughly chopped
1 large potato, peeled and roughly chopped
600ml hot vegetable stock, made with stock cubes
600ml full-fat milk
500g fresh spinach leaves
Finely grated zest of ½ unwaxed lemon, plus
  extra to serve
Salt and freshly ground black pepper

1. Melt the butter in a large saucepan, add the onion and fry gently for 5 minutes until softened, stirring occasionally with a wooden spoon. Add in the potato and cook for a further 3 minutes. Pour in the stock and simmer for 10 minutes, stirring occasionally.

2. Pour in the milk, bring to a boil and gently simmer for 2 minutes, then add half the spinach, lemon zest and season with salt and pepper. Cover and gently simmer for 15 minutes with the lid off.

3. Remove the pan from the heat and add the remaining spinach. With a hand blender, blitz the soup until smooth.

4. Serve immediately while hot, or serve at room temperature the day after for your lunch at the office, with a sprinkling of lemon zest.

Mushroom soup with Marsala wine / VELLUTATA DI PORCINI CON MARSALA

We grow mushrooms all over Italy but especially in high valleys. The best places are the valleys of Piedmont, Lombardy and Veneto. Trentino, Liguria and Emilia-Romagna are also key areas. Of course, Borgotaro in the north is famous for its beautiful porcini mushrooms – if you can, try to use the fresh ones, although the dried ones work well here.

Serves 4

10g dried porcini mushrooms
50g salted butter
3 white onions, peeled and sliced
300g chestnut mushrooms, roughly chopped
300g cup mushrooms, roughly chopped
Salt and white pepper to taste
800ml hot vegetable stock, made with stock cubes
6 tablespoons Marsala wine
1 teaspoon fresh thyme leaves
200ml double cream

1. Place the porcini mushrooms in a small bowl and pour over 200ml warm water. Leave to soak for 20 minutes.

2. Melt the butter in a saucepan over a medium heat and fry the onions for 5 minutes until softened. Stir occasionally with a wooden spoon. Add the chestnut and cup mushrooms and continue to fry for 2 minutes.

3. Drain the porcini mushrooms, reserving their soaking liquid, then squeeze them in your hands to remove any more liquid. Add the mushrooms to the pan and season with salt and pepper. Cook for 8 minutes with the lid on, stirring occasionally. Pour in the stock, the reserved porcini soaking liquid, Marsala wine and thyme. Bring to the boil and simmer for a further 10 minutes.

4. Remove the pan from the heat and blitz until smooth with a hand blender. Slowly pour in the cream while you blitz the soup. Return to the heat and bring to the boil before serving.

Artichoke and lemon soup / ZUPPA
DI CARCIOFI E LIMONE

Most regions in Italy grow artichokes for local use, but in the north the delicious Castraura is a specialty of the Venetian lagoons and the beautiful purple Violetto artichoke from Tuscany adds colour to any dish. In Italy we adore artichokes and use them in many different ways. In this recipe use tinned artichokes in brine and not those in olive oil. They are much cheaper and as the veg need to be drained anyway, you'd only be pouring the precious oil down the sink!

Serves 6

50g salted butter
3 leeks, roughly chopped
1 celery stick, roughly chopped
1.2 litres vegetable stock, made with stock cubes
Juice and zest of 1 unwaxed lemon
2 potatoes, peeled and roughly chopped
2 tablespoons chopped fresh flat leaf parsley
Salt and ground white pepper to taste
2 x 390g tins artichoke hearts in brine, drained
   and cut into quarters
170ml double cream

1. Melt the butter in a large saucepan over a medium heat. Add the leeks and fry for 5 minutes until softened but not browned, stirring occasionally. Add the celery and continue to cook for a further 5 minutes.

2. Pour in the stock, lemon juice and zest, potatoes and parsley and season with salt and pepper. Bring to the boil, then reduce the heat, half-cover the pan with a lid and leave to simmer for 20 minutes, stirring occasionally. Then add the artichokes and cook for a further 10 minutes.

3. Remove the saucepan from the heat and use a hand blender to blitz until smooth. Stir in the cream then reheat gently. Serve in warm deep bowls with plenty of crusty bread.

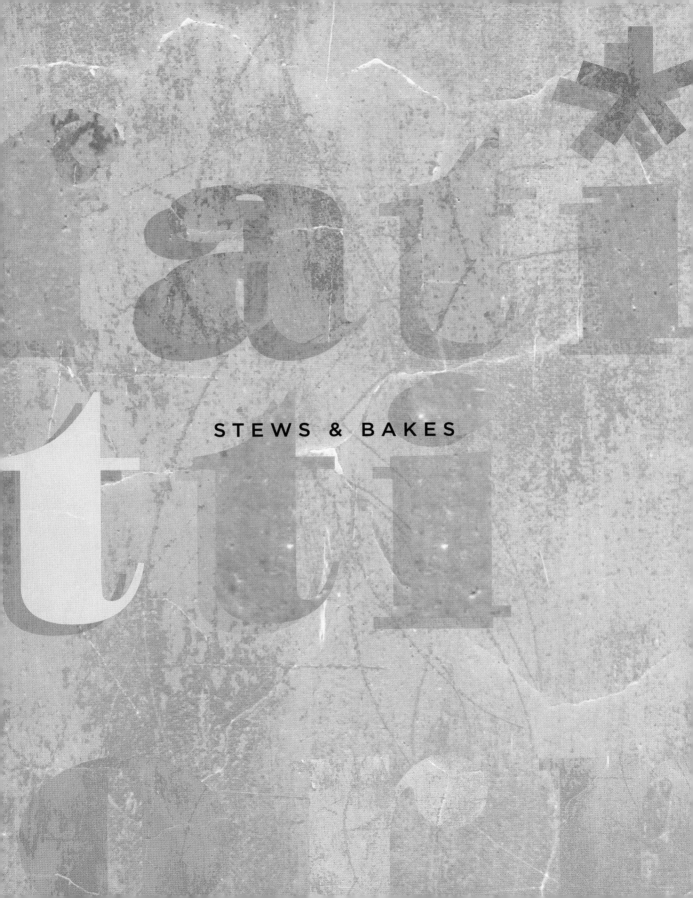

STEWS & BAKES

There is nothing quite as comforting as a hearty baked dish or a steaming bowl of stew, and for some reason when I was travelling through the north of Italy in the summer, a home-made stew always seemed to remind me of home. For some, this might be normal, but for me, who has lived half my life in Naples where we hardly ever had stew because the climate is too hot, and the other half in London where, again, stews are eaten but not necessarily on a regular basis, this dish should have been a novelty. So how could it remind me of home?

I realised that it's not the dish itself that makes you think of home, but the ingredients. It is these that play a major role in providing comfort, alongside the sensation of eating warm hearty food that makes you feel so satisfied. I was lucky enough to try some fabulous creations on my travels and I just love the fact that my taste buds continue to experience new flavours all the time. I have brought some ideas back with me from my trip which I have shared with you in this chapter.

The sauces in Italian stews can range in texture from thin, watery broths to a thickness similar to that of mashed potatoes. In general, Italian stews contain many types of meat and vegetables and tend to be cooked using low-heat methods – on the stove, in the oven, or in a slow cooker. The vegetables cooked in this type of stew are many, but the most popular ones are carrots, celery, fennel, potatoes, onion and often pulses or beans – or even bread. In northern Italy, most stews are cooked with wine, too, which to me is a must!

Bakes, on the other hand, have always been constant in my life. Pasta bakes were especially popular during my childhood as they could be prepared in the morning or even the day before. But it was while travelling in Bologna, Modena and Florence, in particular, that I really had the opportunity to sample a completely different concept of baked dishes. Here I have chosen some of my favourites – and I am sure you will absolutely love them.

Baked citrus sea bass / SPIGOLA AL
FORNO CON ARANCE E LIMONI

A superb, sweet, white fish – sea bass is one of the best-loved fish in Italy. It is versatile, easy to cook and widely available and is by far my favourite fish. If you can't get sea bass, replace it with sea bream.

Serves 6

4 tablespoons olive oil
6 garlic cloves, peeled and thinly sliced
2 fennel bulbs, cored and cut into ½cm slices
1 unwaxed lemon, cut into 2cm chunks
1 orange, cut into 2cm chunks
2 red chillies
6 sea bass fillets (about 180g each)
Salt
2 tablespoons extra virgin olive oil

1. Preheat the oven to 180°C/gas mark 4. Pour the olive oil into a large roasting dish and add the garlic and fennel slices and lemon and orange chunks. Split the chillies from their stalks and add, whole, to the dish. Place the dish in the oven and bake for 30 minutes, stirring halfway through.

2. Slash the skin of the fish fillets four times and season well with salt. Lay the fish on top of the vegetables, skin side up. Drizzle over the extra virgin olive oil and return the dish to the oven for a further 20 minutes.

3. Serve immediately with Tuscan-style roasted potatoes with red onions (see page 200).

Whole roasted sea bream with potatoes and samphire / ORATA

ARROSTO CON PATATE E SALICORNIA

Rock samphire grows everywhere on Italy's coastline, but for this recipe I used marsh samphire – which you can find fresh from your fishmonger or fish counter, or dried and in packets. The saltiness of the samphire complements the sweetness of the fish perfectly. If you can't find sea bream, sea bass will work just as well.

Serves 4

6 large potatoes, peeled and cut into 2cm chunks
4 whole garlic cloves
2 unwaxed lemons, 1 cut into 2cm chunks and
  1 thinly sliced
6 fresh oregano sprigs
Salt and freshly ground black pepper
6 tablespoons extra virgin olive oil
2kg whole sea bream
150ml Italian white wine
100g samphire, rinsed well under cold water

1. Preheat the oven to 240°C/gas mark 9. Place the potatoes and garlic in a large saucepan and cover with cold water. Bring to the boil and simmer for 10 minutes. Drain, and transfer to a mixing bowl with the lemon chunks, the leaves of 3 of the oregano sprigs, salt and pepper and 3 tablespoons of oil. Mix to coat all the potatoes and transfer to a large roasting dish.

2. Run a sharp knife along the belly of the fish and carefully open it up. Stuff the belly with the lemon slices and the remaining oregano sprigs. Season inside and out with salt and pepper. Lay the fish on top of the potatoes and drizzle with the remaining olive oil. Transfer the dish to the oven and roast for 20 minutes.

3. Remove the tray from the oven, pour in the wine and scatter the samphire over the potatoes and fish. Gently turn the potatoes then return to the oven and roast for a further 10 minutes. The fish is cooked properly when you can remove the skin and bones very easily.

4. Fillet the fish. Remove the head and then run a sharp knife along the spine from head to tail, working the blade between the spine and the flesh. If the knife does not go through the flesh easily, the fish is not cooked. Lift the fillet away from the ribs carefully to keep it whole. Turn the fish over and repeat on the other side. Divide the fillets among four serving plates, then serve immediately with the potatoes and a large bottle of cold Italian white wine.

Crispy chicken baked with lemon and fennel / POLLO AL FORNO CON LIMONI E FINOCCHI

It just doesn't get simpler than this – but it looks so impressive when it comes out of the oven. This is a great dish to feed a crowd as the quantities can easily be doubled or trebled, depending on how many guests you have. I have tried this recipe with oranges instead of lemons, too, and it works just as well.

Serves 6

3 large fennel bulbs, cut into quarters, core removed, then each length cut in half again
2 large lemons, cut into ½cm slices
3 medium onions, peeled and cut into ½cm slices
2 tablespoons fresh thyme leaves
6 large chicken thighs, skin on
1 teaspoon salt and freshly ground black pepper
3 tablespoons extra virgin olive oil

1. Preheat the oven to 200°C/gas mark 6. Combine the fennel, lemon and onion slices in a large baking tray with the thyme leaves. Nestle the chicken thighs between the vegetables, skin side up. Season with salt and black pepper and drizzle with olive oil then roast for 1 hour or until the chicken is cooked through – the skin should be crisp and golden brown.

2. Serve hot with rice or sauté potatoes, or at room temperature the day after.

Chicken breasts in mascarpone sauce / PETTI DI POLLO CON SALSA AL MASCARPONE

Chicken is the most common source of meat in the world. Some would say it is a tasteless meat, but they haven't tried this dish yet! This recipe was one of my favourites as a child – perhaps it's the simplicity that appealed to me. Mascarpone cheese is a speciality of Lombardy and is used a lot in northern Italian cooking, but if you can't find it you can replace it with a thick double cream – it doesn't have quite the same flavour or texture, but it will do the job.

Serves 6

1 large onion, peeled and roughly chopped
6 tablespoons chilli-flavoured olive oil
2 x 400g tins chopped tomatoes
1 teaspoon salt
1 teaspoon sugar
250g mascarpone cheese
10 fresh basil leaves, roughly chopped
6 large boneless chicken breasts, skin on
Salt and white pepper to taste

1. Preheat the oven to 180°C/gas mark 4. In a medium saucepan, fry the onion in 4 tablespoons of chilli oil for 5 minutes, stirring occasionally. Pour in the tomatoes with the salt and sugar, bring to the boil and simmer very gently for 10 minutes with the lid on, then 10 minutes with the lid off. Stir occasionally with a wooden spoon.

2. Take the saucepan off the heat and blitz until smooth with a hand blender. Stir in the mascarpone with the basil and set aside.

3. Season the chicken breasts well with salt and pepper. Heat the remaining chilli oil in a large frying pan and fry the chicken on a high heat on both sides until golden brown. Don't move the chicken around or it won't take on any colour.

4. Pour the sauce into an ovenproof dish then place the chicken breasts, skin side up, on top and cook in the oven for 30 minutes or until the chicken is cooked through. Serve with roasted new potatoes and green beans of your choice.

Stewed neck of lamb in thyme and red wine sauce / STUFATO DI AGNELLO CON TIMO E VINO ROSSO

This definitely feels like winter food to me. I've used neck fillet as it's a cheap cut and widely available, but if for some reason you can't get it, any stewing lamb will do. Slow-cooking the lamb will ensure that the meat is meltingly soft and makes it a dish you can prepare the day before your dinner party. *Buon appetito!*

Serves 6

6 tablespoons olive oil
900g lamb neck fillet, cut into 3cm cubes
2 large onions, peeled and finely chopped
75g pitted black olives in oil or brine, drained
2 bay leaves
Juice and grated zest of 1 orange
5 fresh thyme sprigs
350ml red wine
400ml hot vegetable stock, made with stock cubes
1 x 400g tin chopped tomatoes
1 tablespoon runny honey
Salt and freshly ground black pepper to taste

1. Preheat the oven to 150°C/gas mark 2. Heat the oil in a large, flameproof casserole dish and fry the meat in batches until seared and browned on all sides – don't move it around the pan too much or it won't colour. Remove with a slotted spoon and set aside.

2. Add the onions to the same dish and gently fry for 10 minutes, stirring occasionally, until softened. Add the olives, bay leaves, orange juice and zest and thyme and continue to cook for 1 minute.

3. Pour in the wine and cook for 2 minutes, to allow the alcohol to evaporate. Stir occasionally with a wooden spoon. Pour over the vegetable stock, tomatoes and honey and give it a good stir. Bring to the boil then return the meat to the pan. Season with salt and pepper and mix all together.

4. Place a lid on the dish, transfer to the oven and cook for 3 hours. Serve with lots of bread and a salad of your choice.

Slow-cooked veal casserole /

STINCO DI VITELLO IN CASSERUOLA

Veal shin is taken from the part of leg where the muscle is particularly thick and tough, so it needs long, slow cooking to create a soft stew-like meal. This is a fantastic dish for entertaining as everything can be prepared ahead, leaving you time to spend with your friends instead of cooking.

Serves 6

1 large veal shin or pieces of shin (about 1½kg in total)
Salt and freshly ground black pepper
6 tablespoons olive oil
1 large onion, peeled and finely chopped
2 carrots, peeled and roughly chopped
4 celery sticks, roughly chopped
200ml Italian dry white wine
1 x 400g tin chopped tomatoes
3 fresh rosemary sprigs
Zest of 1 unwaxed lemon
1 garlic clove, peeled and crushed
4 tablespoons chopped fresh flat leaf parsley

1. Preheat the oven to 150°C/gas mark 2. Season the veal with salt and pepper. Heat the oil in a large ovenproof saucepan and fry the veal on all sides for 5 minutes to brown it – don't move it around the pan too much or it won't colour. Remove from the saucepan with a slotted spoon and set aside.

2. Add the onion, carrots and celery to the same saucepan and fry for 10 minutes until softened, scraping all the caramelised bits off the bottom of the pan with a wooden spoon. Pour in the wine and cook for 2 minutes, allowing the alcohol to evaporate. Tip in the tomatoes and rosemary and bring to the boil, then return the meat to the pan, cover with a lid and transfer to the oven to cook for 3 hours. Stir the casserole every hour.

3. Meanwhile, combine the lemon zest, garlic and parsley in a small bowl. Set aside.

4. Divide the veal between four serving plates and sprinkle over the lemon, garlic and parsley mixture. Serve immediately with a little rice on the side.

Chicken and porcini mushroom casserole / CASSERUOLA DI POLLO CON PORCINI

This is the recipe of romance. The only thing you need to go with it is warm crusty bread, a big salad and someone to love. Get cosy with a warm Italian casserole. Where's my wife?

Serves 6

25g dried porcini mushrooms
200ml warm water
5 tablespoons olive oil
6 medium skinless, boneless chicken breasts
1 large onion, peeled and finely chopped
2 carrots, peeled and finely chopped
2 celery sticks, finely chopped
150g cup mushrooms, roughly chopped
150ml Italian white wine
1 x 400g tin chopped tomatoes
100ml passata (sieved tomatoes)
200ml hot chicken stock, made with stock cubes
1 teaspoon caster sugar
1 tablespoon fresh oregano leaves, roughly chopped
Fresh flat leaf parsley to garnish

1. Preheat the oven to 180°C/gas mark 4. Place the porcini mushrooms in a bowl, pour over the warm water and leave to soak for 20 minutes.

2. Heat the oil in a large, flameproof casserole dish over a medium heat and fry the chicken breasts for 8 minutes until they are brown all over. Do not move them around or they will not take on any colour. Remove with a slotted spoon and set aside.

3. Add the onion, carrots, celery and cup mushrooms to the casserole dish and fry for 10 minutes over a gentle heat, stirring occasionally.

4. Drain the porcini mushrooms, reserving their soaking liquid, then squeeze them in your hands to remove any more liquid. Finely chop the mushrooms and add to the casserole dish together with the reserved soaking liquid, wine, tinned tomatoes, passata, stock, sugar and oregano. Return the chicken to the dish along with its juices. Bring to the boil, cover with a lid and transfer to the oven to cook for 45 minutes.

5. Serve on a large serving plate garnished with chopped flat leaf parsley.

Tuscan baked fennel / FINOCCHI AL FORNO ALLA TOSCANA

I'm always impressed whenever I'm served a gratin, even though I know that it is really simple to prepare. Fennel works so well in a gratin but cauliflower, carrots or any root vegetable are just as delicious here. If you prefer, replace the Parmesan cheese with Pecorino cheese.

Serves 4

600g fennel bulbs
Salt and freshly ground black pepper
1 unwaxed lemon, cut in half
1 tablespoon extra virgin olive oil
50g salted butter
30g freshly grated Parmesan cheese

1. Cut the fennel bulbs vertically into 1cm thick slices, leaving the core intact – this will hold the leaves together. Place in a medium saucepan with a teaspoon of salt, the lemon halves and oil. Cover with boiling water and simmer for 15 minutes. Drain and set aside.

2. Heat the grill to medium. Put the butter in a shallow flameproof dish and melt it under the grill. Remove and add the fennel slices, turning to coat in the butter. Season with salt and pepper then sprinkle over the Parmesan and return to the grill for 5 minutes until the cheese is melted and bubbling.

3. Serve immediately on a large serving plate surrounded by a selection of your favourite cheeses and crunchy bread.

Baked polenta with oozing Gorgonzola / POLENTA AL FORNO CON GORGONZOLA FUSO

Restaurants and hotels in Italy were once ashamed to offer polenta on the menus, as it had been labelled as food for the poor in the 1950s, but after many years of neglect this maize-flour ingredient has made a dramatic comeback. Polenta is now very fashionable in the north of Italy, especially in Veneto, where it was once a staple ingredient. If you have never tried polenta please give this recipe a go, you won't regret it.

Serves 6

2 teaspoons salt
375g quick-cook polenta
100g salted butter
1 teaspoon freshly ground white pepper
3 tablespoons chopped fresh chives
250g Gorgonzola cheese, cold and cut into
  small pieces

1. Preheat the oven to 200°C/gas mark 6. Heat 1.5 litres of water in a medium saucepan with a little salt and bring to the boil. Little by little, pour in the polenta, stirring continuously. Turn the heat down to low and continue to cook and stir for 8 minutes. Please use a wooden spoon for this – it will make your life easier.

2. Take the pan off the heat and stir in the butter, white pepper and chives. Immediately pour half the polenta into a 28 x 20cm baking tray with sides at least 6cm high and spread it out evenly. If you leave the polenta it will become too hard to spread, so work quickly. Sprinkle over half of the Gorgonzola pieces and pour over the remaining polenta. Dot the remaining Gorgonzola over the top to finish.

3. Bake in the oven for 25 minutes. The polenta should be crispy on top and soft and creamy in the middle, with the melted Gorgonzola oozing through.

77

Spicy cannellini bean and spinach stew / STUFATO PICCANTE DI FAGIOLI E SPINACI

Cumin is a spice similar to aniseed, which grows around the edges of fields all over the north-east of Italy in summer. This dish can be served as a filling vegetarian main, but I usually make it as an accompaniment. Feel free to grate some Parmesan cheese over the top to make it extra special.

Serves 4

1 tablespoon olive oil
1 large onion, peeled and finely chopped
1 teaspoon dried chilli flakes
1 teaspoon ground cumin
1 x 400g tin chopped tomatoes
1 teaspoon caster sugar
¼ teaspoon salt
1 x 400g tin cannellini beans, drained
120g green beans, roughly chopped
100g fresh spinach, roughly chopped

1. Heat the oil in a medium saucepan and gently fry the onion with the chilli flakes for 6 minutes, stirring occasionally, until the onion has softened. Add the cumin and cook for a further minute. Pour in the tomatoes, sugar, salt and 200ml water, bring to the boil then simmer gently for 10 minutes, uncovered. Stir it occasionally.

2. Add the cannellini beans and green beans and cook for a further 5 minutes. Finally, add the spinach and cook for 5 minutes longer.

3. Perfect served with crusty bread and a large glass of Italian red wine.

FISH & SEAFOOD

Anywhere you travel to in the north of Italy will never be too far away from the sea or lakes. In spite of the long coastline, though, the cuisine of this region has fewer fish dishes than one might expect. One of the reasons for this is that during springtime, when fish are reproducing, there is a ban on fishing (this is true not just in Italy, but everywhere). Even in the other months of the year, though, fish was still not abundant as it was often difficult to transport fresh fish inland quickly before it was past its best.

Personally I think the culinary options in the north are more geared towards meats and rice – which are still the number one choice for northern Italians. But although fish and seafood are

definitely not as popular here as they are in the south, they are always an option on most menus and the recipes are always fantastic in flavour.

There are also areas in the region that have created their own specialities based on local produce. The cuisine of Venice, for instance, is rich in molluscs, crustaceans, sardines and other fish that inhabit the lagoon. Liguria is famous for its fish stew and baccala – salt cod or dried cod, which are always available and have become two of the main components of the local cuisine. It's funny because for decades preserved cod has always been plentiful and was very cheap, but now it has become hugely popular and quite an expensive ingredient. There are also regions

82

renowned for their eels, while the coastal lowlands will provide swordfish, sardines and sea bass. So although fish might not be top of the northern Italian cuisine list, when it is prepared its quality definitely makes it top for most of the visiting tourists – which includes me. One of the most popular fish that you will almost definitely find on the menu for all antipasti options are fresh-caught anchovies. These are often served very simply –

extremely fresh with a hint of lemon – and are a must-try. I have used them in quite a few of my recipes as the salty flavour really enhances many dishes. Here I have chosen a selection of fish recipes which I absolutely love – some may shock you, but please try them. *Buon appetito!*

Slow-cooked squid in a spicy tomato sauce / CALAMARI AL SUGO DI POMODORO PICCANTE

Before you panic when reading this recipe, it really isn't as gory to prepare as it sounds and if you really are squeamish, get your fishmonger to help rather than bypass this dish – it really is worth it. I have often served this sauce with pasta but I still prefer to have warm crusty bread to go with it. It also makes a *fantastico* starter.

Serves 6

800g fresh squid
120ml olive oil
3 garlic cloves, peeled and crushed
1 teaspoon dried chilli flakes
2 tablespoons capers in salt, rinsed under cold
   water and drained
100g pitted green olives, drained and cut in half
250ml dry white wine
2 x 400g tins chopped tomatoes
3 tablespoons chopped fresh flat leaf parsley
Salt to taste

1. To prepare the squid, first pull away the tentacles from the body then remove the quill (which looks like a long piece of clear plastic). Pull the wings away from the body, peel off the membrane and set aside. Peel away the thin purple membrane coating the body of the squid. Turn the squid inside out and wash under cold running water. Set aside. Cut the tentacles away from the head just behind the eyes, then pull out the hard beak and discard. Slice the body of the squid into 1cm rings and the wings into 1cm thick slices.

2. Heat the oil in a medium saucepan over a medium heat and fry the garlic, chilli, capers and olives for 30 seconds. Add in the squid and fry for a further 8 minutes so that the water is released. Stir occasionally with a wooden spoon. Pour in the wine and continue to cook for a further 2 minutes, allowing the alcohol to evaporate. Tip in the chopped tomatoes and bring to the boil. Lower the heat, mix in the parsley and simmer, uncovered, for 1 hour, stirring with a wooden spoon every 10 minutes.

3. Season with salt and serve hot with lots of crusty bread to mop up the sauce. A large glass of cold Italian white wine is also a must with this...

Braised scallops with peas and sun-dried tomatoes / CAPESANTE
BRASATE CON PISELLI E POMODORI SECCHI

I adore scallops and must admit that I don't like to interfere by adding too many ingredients that will alter their natural flavour, but I really think this recipe is special. It is so simple and quick to prepare and is very flexible in terms of being great as a dinner for one, or a starter or a main at a dinner party. You can replace the pancetta with chorizo if you prefer, and of course the fresher the scallops the better.

Serves 4

3 tablespoons extra virgin olive oil
100g diced pancetta
16 spring onions, chopped into 5cm chunks
500g frozen peas, defrosted
2 heads baby gem lettuce, cut into 2cm pieces
60g salted butter
100g sun-dried tomatoes in oil, drained and
    finely sliced
12 small scallops, without the coral
Salt and white pepper to taste

1. Heat the oil in a large frying pan and fry the pancetta for 3 minutes over a medium heat. Stir occasionally with a wooden spoon.

2. Add the spring onions to the frying pan. Cook for 3 minutes then add the peas and enough water to cover the lot. Simmer for 4 minutes. Add in the chopped baby gem lettuce with the butter and sun-dried tomatoes and continue to simmer for 2 minutes. Add the scallops and simmer for a further 1½ minutes.

3. Divide among four warm shallow bowls, season and serve immediately. Fresh rustic bread is a must with this recipe to mop up all the delicious juices.

Octopus and potatoes with lemon and chilli / POLPO E PATATE CON LIMONE E PEPERONCINO

Octopus is really big in the south of Italy, where I am from. We often just simply barbecue or fry it – but I love the way the northern Italians boil it and serve it cold in salads with potatoes. It really works and you can add any kind of dressing to it. You will find this octopus salad everywhere in the north, and not just in Venice, where I tried it. It appears on all menus, from the very finest restaurants to the simplest café. It is a definite must-try.

Serves 4

1 small octopus (about 500g)
2 celery sticks, cut into 1cm pieces
1 small red onion, peeled and kept whole
1 large fresh chilli
Juice and zest of 1 unwaxed lemon
Salt and black pepper to taste
2 tablespoons capers in vinegar or brine, rinsed and drained
8 tablespoons extra virgin olive oil
700g small yellow waxy potatoes, peeled
6 tablespoons fresh flat leaf parsley leaves, left whole

1. Place the whole octopus into a medium saucepan and add in the celery, onion, whole chilli and lemon zest. Cover with cold water and bring to the boil, then turn down the heat to a very low simmer and cook, half-covered, for 1 hour. Remove from the heat and leave the octopus to cool in the liquid.

2. Once the octopus is completely cool, remove from the cooking liquid, cut into 3cm pieces and place in a large bowl. Season with salt and pepper, add in the capers and pour over the lemon juice with 4 tablespoons of olive oil. Mix everything together and set aside at room temperature.

3. Meanwhile, bring a large pan of salted water to the boil. Cook the potatoes for 20 minutes, drain, then cut into quarters. Place the chopped potatoes in a large clean bowl, season with salt and pepper and drizzle over 4 tablespoons of olive oil. Add the parsley leaves and mix together.

4. Serve the potatoes at room temperature on a large plate with the octopus and plenty of warm crusty bread.

Potato and smoked salmon crocchette / CROCCHETTE DI PATATE E SALMONE AFFUMICATO

This is a winner for adults with a chilled glass of white wine, but it is also a firm favourite with the kids. Forget about fish fingers and get them to make these with you. The shapes they create might be a bit skewwhiff but they will have fun and eat them like biscuits once they are ready. I have made these as a snack, to accompany a dish and as a starter, and they never disappoint. You can replace the smoked salmon with kippers or even ham if you want to experiment.

Makes 12 crocchette

4 large floury potatoes, Maris Piper or King Edward (about 300g)
100g freshly grated Parmesan cheese
2 tablespoons chopped fresh flat leaf parsley
1 egg, beaten
80g smoked salmon, cut into very small pieces
200g instant polenta
1 litre vegetable oil or sunflower oil for deep-frying
Salt and white pepper to taste
1 lemon, cut into four wedges

1. Place the potatoes, skin on, in a large saucepan with 1 tablespoon of salt. Cover with water and bring to the boil. Cook for 30 minutes until softened, then drain and, when cool enough to handle, peel and put them through a ricer while still warm.

2. Place the potato mixture in a large mixing bowl with the Parmesan, parsley, egg and the salmon. Mix well and shape the mixture into 12 slightly elongated balls – like a short sausage. Roll in the polenta and set aside until ready to cook.

3. Half-fill a deep pan with the oil and start to heat it. The perfect oil temperature should be 190°C. Test it by dropping in a cube of bread – it should turn golden in less than a minute. Deep-fry the crocchette in the hot oil for 2 minutes until golden and beautiful. Drain on kitchen paper and season with salt and pepper.

4. Serve immediately on a large warm serving platter surrounded by the lemon wedges.

Pan-fried sea bass with cannellini mash and basil sauce/

SPIGOLA CON PURÉ DI CANNELLINI E SALSA AL BASILICO

It has often been said that beans are the meat of the poor man, as they are a healthy alternative to meat, but in Italy, beans are used in pasta dishes, salads, mashed and spread on bruschetta – to name but a few options. They are used all day every day and are so incredibly good for you – packed with protein and soluble fibre, they make a really wonderful alternative to potatoes. The creamy bean mash here will not disappoint and complements the sea bass and the fresh basil sauce perfectly.

Serves 4

4 sea bass fillets (about 200g each), skin on
Salt and white pepper to taste
40g plain flour for dusting
4 tablespoons olive oil

For the basil sauce
110ml olive oil
30g fresh basil leaves, plus a few small leaves
    to serve
1 tablespoon capers in brine, drained
4 anchovy fillets in oil, drained
1 garlic clove, peeled
Squeeze of lemon juice

For the cannellini mash
6 tablespoons olive oil
1 garlic clove, peeled and finely chopped
2 x 400g tins cannellini beans, drained

1. Prepare the cannellini mash by pouring the oil in a medium saucepan then add the garlic and fry for 20 seconds. Add the beans and cook on a medium heat for 10 minutes, stirring occasionally. If the mixture appears to be dry, add a little hot water. Season with salt and pepper and use a potato masher to gently crush the beans. Cover to keep warm and set aside.

2. For the basil sauce, place all the ingredients in a food processor or blender and blitz until smooth. Season with salt and pepper and set aside.

3. Cut each fish fillet in half, season with salt and pepper and lightly flour both sides. Heat 4 tablespoons of olive oil in a large frying pan over a medium heat and fry the fish, skin side down, for 3 minutes. Gently turn each fillet over and cook for a further 2 minutes – the fish is ready when firm to the touch but not dry.

4. Put equal amounts of the cannellini mash in the centre of 4 warm serving plates, place the fish fillets on top, drizzle over the basil sauce and scatter over the reserved basil leaves. Serve immediately.

Fresh cod and red onion frittata

/ FRITTATA DI MERLUZZO E CIPOLLE ROSSE

We have all made a frittata with leftovers before but everyone thought I was really taking a risk with this combination. I figured if you can have scrambled eggs and smoked salmon then why not a delicate cod for example? Boy am I glad I didn't listen to everyone, as this knock-up concoction is fantastic. If you have children that aren't big fish eaters, try this – they won't even realise till it's too late that they are having the healthiest, tastiest omelette ever. If they like it, experiment with salmon or trout too instead of the cod. When a risk or accident becomes such a huge culinary success, it deserves to be in my top ten fish chapter.

Serves 6

400g cod fillet, skin and bones removed
8 eggs
4 tablespoons chopped fresh chives
Salt and black pepper to taste
100ml extra virgin olive oil
1 large red onion, peeled and thinly sliced
500g potatoes, peeled and cut into 2cm chunks

1. Place the cod in a medium saucepan and cover with water. Bring to the boil and simmer for 8 minutes. Lift out the fish and when cool enough to handle, break into large flakes. Set aside.

2. Beat the eggs in a large bowl with the chives. Season with salt and pepper and set aside.

3. Pour the oil into a 22cm non-stick frying pan and place over a medium heat. Fry the onion for 4 minutes until softened, stirring occasionally with a wooden spoon. Add in the potatoes, season with salt and pepper and continue to cook for a further 15 minutes until tender, stirring occasionally. Add the fish to the pan and mix everything together. Pour over the egg mixture and cook on a low heat for 15 minutes.

4. Meanwhile, preheat the grill to high. Place the frying pan under the hot grill for 3 minutes to allow the frittata to set and turn a fantastic, light brown colour.

5. Transfer the frittata to a large flat serving plate and cut into wedges. Serve hot or warm with your favourite salad.

Roasted monkfish wrapped in Parma ham / CODA DI ROSPO AVVOLTA IN PROSCIUTTO CRUDO

Monkfish are known to be very ugly, so the actual translation of *coda di rospo* is 'fishing frog' or 'toad's tail'. Many fishmongers skin them and sell just the tail ends, which is the most edible part. It's funny how their looks still won't stop anyone buying this amazing fish. All the ingredients I have added to the recipe really enhance the flavour of the fish and just combine to be a match made in heaven – hope you agree.

Serves 4

100g salted butter
2 red onions, peeled and sliced
800g new potatoes, skin on and cut into quarters
Salt and black pepper to taste
3 tablespoons fresh rosemary leaves
2 garlic cloves, peeled
8 anchovy fillets in oil, drained
5 tablespoons chopped fresh flat leaf parsley
60g fresh white breadcrumbs
4 tablespoons extra virgin olive oil
1kg monkfish tail, cut into 4 fillets
16 slices of Parma ham

1. Preheat the oven to 200°C/gas mark 6. Grease a large roasting tray with half the butter and tip in the onions and potatoes. Season well with salt and pepper, sprinkle over the rosemary and dot with the remaining butter. Roast in the middle of the oven for 30 minutes until cooked through and golden, shaking the tray every 10 minutes.

2. Meanwhile, place the garlic, anchovies, parsley and breadcrumbs in a food processor or crush in a pestle and mortar. Pour in 2 tablespoons of oil, season with salt and pepper and blitz until well mixed. If it looks too dry, add a little more oil.

3. Lay two monkfish fillets flat side up on a chopping board and spread the parsley mixture over. Place the remaining fillets on top to create two parcels. Wrap the Parma ham around each parcel and tie with string at 2cm intervals. Remove the roasting tray from the oven, place the monkfish parcels on top of the potatoes and roast for 25 minutes more.

4. Place the roasted monkfish on a chopping board and cut each parcel into four chunks. Divide the potatoes between four warm serving plates and place two chunks of monkfish on top. Serve hot with a beautiful glass of Italian red wine.

Lemon-dressed raw langoustines

/ MAZZANCOLLE ALLA CRUDAIOLA CON LIMONE

This recipe is for people who love the natural flavours of fish. This dish is so fresh that it almost swims to the table. With no cooking whatsoever involved, it doesn't get much healthier than this. It is really quick to prepare and also makes this a fantastic antipasti option. If you prefer you can toss the langoustines into a salad, but serving them the way I suggest here just looks really impressive and that little bit more special.

Serves 4

20 live langoustines
½ teaspoon dried chilli flakes
Sea salt to taste
½ teaspoon dried oregano
Extra virgin olive oil
2 lemons, cut into wedges

1. Place a large serving platter in the fridge 30 minutes before you need to serve the langoustines. After 15 minutes, place the langoustines in the freezer.

2. Place the chilled langoustines on a large chopping board, belly side up. Hold them carefully with your hand protected by a cloth. Use a large sharp knife to cut through the head and then down the centre to open them up, butterfly style. Arrange the opened langoustines, belly side up, on the cold serving platter.

3. Sprinkle over the chilli flakes, salt and oregano. Generously drizzle over the olive oil and serve immediately with wedges of lemon around the chilled platter. Accompany the raw langoustines with warm crusty bread and a little mixed salad on the side.

Whole salmon with roasted peppers, potatoes and anchovies

/ SALMONE AL FORNO CON PATATE, PEPERONI E ACCIUGHE

Salmon is not an Italian fish and yet it is found in abundance on the fresh fish market stalls all over the country. The trend in the north seems to be to roast the fish whole – and I must agree, I do love salmon cooked this way or in pastry parcels. There is something really special about serving a whole fish to your guests; when you plate it, it looks so fantastic and you will always get a 'wow'. Use trout if you prefer a milder-tasting fish.

Serves 4

1kg waxy potatoes, peeled and sliced into
   1cm slices
Sea salt and black pepper to taste
5 large plum tomatoes, cut into quarters
   lengthways
4 yellow peppers, deseeded and cut into eight
60g anchovy fillets in oil, drained
6 garlic cloves, peeled and cut in half
8 fresh rosemary sprigs
160ml vegetable stock
6 tablespoons extra virgin olive oil, plus
   extra for drizzling
1 whole salmon (about 1.5kg)

1. Preheat the oven to 210°C/gas mark 7. Place the potatoes in a large saucepan and cover with water. Add 1 tablespoon of salt, bring to the boil and cook for 5 minutes, then drain.

2. Tip the potato slices into a bowl with the tomatoes, peppers, anchovies, garlic and rosemary and mix together. Arrange the vegetables in a narrow strip over the base of a large roasting dish to make a bed for the salmon. Pour in the stock, season with salt and freshly ground black pepper and then pour over the oil. Bake in the middle of the oven for 30 minutes.

3. Meanwhile, slash the salmon 4 times down each side and then again in the opposite direction on one side to create an attractive criss-cross pattern. Rub it well with more olive oil, season with salt and pepper and place on top of the potato bed. Return the roasting dish to the oven and cook for a further 40 minutes or until the salmon is cooked through.

4. Divide and serve among four warm serving plates accompanied by the roasted vegetables.

Sea bass with capers and butter sauce with griddled carrots /

BRANZINO CON SALSA DI BURRO E CAPPERI E CAROTE GRIGLIATE

Liguria is a beautiful place to go fishing and you can catch some of the best fish in northern Italy there. Sea bass is a really special fish that's packed with flavour and so needs only the simplest cooking, and in this region a popular way to serve it is baked in a salt crust. Here I have cooked the fish with this in mind, serving it with a delicious salty caper sauce.

Serves 4

2 sea bass fillets, pin-boned, skin on
100g plain flour, seasoned with salt and pepper
2 tablespoons olive oil
3 tablespoons butter

For the carrots
3 medium carrots
2–3 tablespoons olive oil, plus extra for drizzling
1 tablespoon salt
1 garlic clove, thinly sliced
10 fresh mint leaves, finely chopped
Pinch of chilli flakes
4 tablespoons white wine vinegar

For the caper butter sauce
3 tablespoons olive oil
2 garlic cloves, finely sliced
50g capers in salt, rinsed and chopped
4 tablespoons fresh flat leaf parsley
60g butter
1 lemon

1. Cook the carrots, whole, in a saucepan of boiling water for 6 minutes. Meanwhile, put a griddle pan on a high heat. Remove the carrots from the pan and plunge into a bowl of iced water. Slice into chunks ½cm thick on the diagonal. Transfer to a bowl and drizzle over the olive oil, a good pinch of salt and toss together.

2. Carefully put the carrot slices on the hot griddle and allow them to char – once you can see griddle lines, turn them over and cook on the other side. Transfer to a bowl and add the garlic, another drizzle of oil, the mint, chilli flakes and vinegar. Toss together and set aside.

3. Make 4 diagonal incisions in the skin of each fish fillet then coat them in the seasoned flour and shake off any excess. Heat the oil and butter in a large frying pan, and once the butter starts to bubble place the fillets skin-side down in the pan, pushing them down so that they crisp up. Cook for 5–6 minutes then turn over the fillets and cook for a further 3 minutes. Remove the fish from the pan and keep warm.

4. Wipe out the pan, add 3 tablespoons oil and heat on a medium heat. Add the garlic and cook for 1 minute then add the capers and parsley. Add the butter, allow to melt then mix it into the other ingredients. Remove from the heat and squeeze in the lemon juice before giving it a final stir.

5. Serve the fillets on individual plates with the carrots, and the sauce spooned over the fish.

PASTA

In any region of Italy pasta will always make up a huge section of the menu, but there are still strong favourites in particular regions.

There are two basic categories of commercial pasta: fresh pasta and dried pasta. By law, fresh pasta must contain 5.5 per cent egg solids by weight. The egg provides a richer colour and flavour – and a few more calories. Dried pasta differs in that it has a slightly nutty flavour, reflecting the durum wheat with which it is made. The classic Italian fresh pastas, such as tagliatelle, fettuccine and lasagne, are flat and of varying width and are also made in non-egg, dried versions. Egg pasta originated in the Emilia-Romagna region of north-central Italy.

Fresh egg-based pasta goes well with hearty dishes and also meat-based or cream sauces. It can be flavoured with spinach (green-coloured), tomato (red-coloured), or squid ink (black-coloured) and is often also used in comfort foods such as casseroles and soups. Italians consider the northerners to be the masters at making fresh pasta, the sheets of which they either cut into strips to make tagliatelle, leave whole to make lasagne or use to make some of the most classic stuffed pastas, including tortellini and cappelletti.

What I did notice on my travels is that although the northern Italians do enjoy pasta, they will often replace it with potatoes, rice or polenta and combine these with simple sauces, of which pesto is perhaps the best known. The north also produces ravioli, which features on most menus of the region, flavoured with various greens and ricotta cheese, although they can also be meat-filled.

Another firm favourite in the north is farfalle (butterfly shape) pasta, which dates back to the 1500s. This shape is very versatile and can be used with most sauces but it is predominantly served with ones that are cream-based or with pesto. Miniature farfalle (farfalline) are made for soups but a strong competitor would be a filled tortellini in a clear broth.

I can eat pasta every day – and many Italians do – so I have tried to pick a varied selection for you and hope I've chosen recipes that will inspire you too. Enjoy!

Bologna-style rigatoni with mortadella and chicken / RIGATONI

AL RAGÙ DI MORTADELLA E POLLO

My younger son Rocco is a huge fan of mortadella so we often have it in the fridge. This chicken dish is quite a traditional recipe from Bologna but including mortadella is a D'Acampo touch. Mortadella is a cured meat that has been eaten by Italians for years. It actually used to be made from cured horse meat but now is made with cured pork, peppercorns and pistachios. It's a fantastic substitute for ham and we love it.

Serves 4

8 tablespoons olive oil
2 large red onions, peeled and finely sliced
½ teaspoon dried chilli flakes
2 large skinless, boneless chicken breasts, cut into 1cm cubes
150g thick slice of mortadella, cut into 1cm cubes
1 x 400g tin chopped tomatoes
10 fresh basil leaves
Salt to taste
500g dried rigatoni
60g freshly grated Pecorino cheese to serve

1. Pour the oil in a medium saucepan over a medium heat and fry the onions for 5 minutes, stirring occasionally with a wooden spoon. Add in the chilli, chicken and mortadella pieces and continue to cook for a further 5 minutes, stirring occasionally. Pour in the chopped tomatoes with the basil leaves, stir well and gently simmer for 10 minutes, uncovered, stirring every couple of minutes. Season with salt and set aside.

2. Meanwhile, cook the pasta in a large saucepan of salted boiling water until al dente. Stir occasionally to prevent it sticking. For the perfect al dente bite, cook the pasta 1 minute less than instructed on the packet. Drain and tip back into the same saucepan. Set the pan over a medium heat, pour over the sauce and stir everything together for 10 seconds, allowing the flavours to combine and the sauce to stick to the pasta.

3. Serve immediately in warm pasta bowls and sprinkle over the Pecorino.

Pasta with rabbit ragù / FUSILLI CON RAGÙ DI CONIGLIO

This recipe is very different and worth a try. The flavours are unique compared to what you and your family are probably used to and it really is a wonderful, rich way to make a ragù. Please, whatever you do, don't just throw away the discarded vegetables, place them in a saucepan with some passata (sieved tomatoes) and heat it through, then you have created a sauce that can be used to top fish baked in foil or that can be served with pasta another time.

Serves 4

4 rabbit legs (about 800g in total)
Salt and black pepper to taste
1 tablespoon salted butter
60ml olive oil
1 carrot, peeled and finely chopped
1 onion, peeled and finely chopped
1 celery stick, finely chopped
1 tablespoon fresh thyme leaves
2 tablespoons tomato purée
80ml white wine
250ml chicken stock, made from stock cubes
2 tablespoons chopped fresh flat leaf parsley
10 cherry tomatoes, cut into quarters
500g fresh fusilli lunghi
80g freshly grated Pecorino cheese to serve

1. Season the rabbit legs and set aside. Melt the butter with the oil in a medium saucepan and fry the rabbit legs for 5 minutes on a medium heat, until browned on all sides. Remove the meat from the saucepan and set aside.

2. Add the carrot, onion and celery to the saucepan with the thyme and fry for 5 minutes until the vegetables have softened, stirring occasionally. Return the rabbit legs to the saucepan with the tomato purée and continue to cook for 2 minutes. Pour in the wine and cook for 2 minutes to allow the alcohol to evaporate. Pour in enough chicken stock to cover all the ingredients in the saucepan, cover with a lid and cook on a low heat for 45 minutes. Every 10 minutes stir the ingredients with a wooden spoon.

3 Remove the rabbit legs and set aside until cool enough to handle. Lightly shred the meat and discard the bones. Strain the stock, discarding the vegetables, and transfer to a clean frying pan. Add the rabbit pieces, parsley and cherry tomatoes to the stock, place over a medium heat and simmer for a few minutes until the sauce is reduced and thick.

4 Bring a large saucepan of salted water to the boil and cook the fresh fusilli for about 3 minutes, until al dente. Drain and return to the saucepan. Place the pan on a medium heat and pour over the rabbit ragù. Mix everything together for 10 seconds, allowing the flavours to combine beautifully and the sauce to stick to the pasta. Check for seasoning one more time and serve immediately with Pecorino sprinkled on top.

My grandfather's tagliatelle with Bolognese sauce / TAGLIATELLE
ALLA BOLOGNESE DI MIO NONNO

This is the real thing. The genuine ragù, as it is made in Bologna, is a mouthwatering meat sauce that includes different types of mince, including pork and beef, slowly cooked in a tomato and vegetable sauce. In Italy, this sauce is only ever served with broad, flat pasta such as tagliatelle or fettuccine, never with spaghetti.

Serves 6

2 tablespoons olive oil
1 onion, very finely diced
2 celery sticks, very finely diced
1 large carrot, very finely diced
500g minced pork
500g minced beef
50ml red wine
50ml milk
4 tablespoons tomato purée
300ml passata
400ml chicken or vegetable stock
500g fresh tagliatelle
Parmesan shavings, to serve (optional)

1. Heat half the oil in a large sauté pan and fry the onion, celery and carrot for 5 minutes until soft and starting to colour.

2. While the vegetables are cooking, put all the meat in a large bowl, pour over the remaining olive oil and crumble the meat between your fingertips. Add the meat to the pan and fry until brown – around 5 minutes.

3. Deglaze the pan with the red wine and allow to simmer for a couple of minutes, then add the milk. Simmer for 2 minutes before stirring in the tomato purée, passata and stock. Simmer gently for 3 hours until reduced and thickened. Once cooked, remove from the hob, season with salt and pepper then cover with a lid and leave for 20 minutes – you do not want the sauce to be boiling hot when you serve it.

4. When ready to serve, bring a large pan of water to the boil and season generously with salt. Add the pasta to the pan and cook for 2–3 minutes or until just cooked. Drain the pasta, then return to the pan with the sauce and toss to combine. Serve in bowls with a few Parmesan shavings scattered over, if you like. Enjoy!

Fresh Ligurian fettuccine / PASTA
FRESCA ALLA LIGURE

If you have ever made your own pasta, you know how rewarding and how easy it is to do. There is nothing nicer than eating a bowl of pasta knowing that everything you are putting into your mouth has been created by you. It's cheaper, healthier and somehow ten times more satisfying. This particular recipe is special; the eggs create a creamier texture and the wine somehow gives it a new dimension. This pasta is perfect served simply with butter and cheese or with a light sauce like pesto.

Serves 6 (makes approx. 1kg)

500g plain '00' flour, plus extra for dusting
1 large egg
3 large egg yolks
40ml dry white wine
3 tablespoons extra virgin olive oil
1 teaspoon fine salt

1. Place the flour in a large bowl, make a well in the centre and break in the whole egg and egg yolks. Pour in the wine and oil and sprinkle over the salt. Using the handle of a wooden spoon, mix the edge of the flour shape into the eggs and stir to combine.

2. Once you have a crumbly texture, tip the mixture onto a well-floured surface and start to knead until you have a large soft dough – this will take about 10 minutes. Roll the dough into a ball, cover with cling film and leave to rest in the fridge for 1 hour.

3. Dust the work surface, the dough and the rolling pin with flour to prevent sticking. Flatten the dough with the palm of your hand, then place the rolling pin across the dough and roll it towards the centre. Continue to roll the pin backwards and forwards, turning the dough every so often. At this point the dough should spread out and flatten evenly. When it is thin enough that you can see your fingers through it, it's ready. Start to roll the pasta sheet like a flattened cigar from one edge to the centre, and then repeat from the other edge to the centre.

4. Make sure that the pasta is well floured, then with a sharp long knife, cut it into 5mm-wide strips. Slide the knife beneath the rolled pasta sheet, lining up the edge of the knife with the centre of the folds. Gently lift the knife so that the pasta ribbons fall down on each side. Toss the ribbons with a little more flour and cook within the hour, in a pan of boiling, salted water for 3–4 minutes until al dente.

Florentine pasta shells stuffed with beef and béchamel sauce /

CONCHIGLIONI RIPIENI ALLA FIORENTINA

If your time is precious and you need to make a delicious dinner in a hurry, this is the perfect recipe. It is a little more special in terms of looks than a traditional Italian pasta bake but it still has the benefit that it can be prepared in advance, leaving you to sort out the kids or come home from work and just put in the oven. If you prepare it ahead, take it out of the fridge 20 minutes before cooking to allow it to come up to room temperature and then place in the oven for an extra 5 minutes with the foil on. This is a really lovely hearty dish – and an elegant one at the same time. You can replace the Grana Padano with Pecorino if you prefer.

Serves 4

24 dried conchiglioni (large pasta shells)
Salt and black pepper to taste
1 tablespoon salted butter
4 tablespoons olive oil
1 red onion, peeled and finely chopped
500g minced beef
1 tablespoon fresh rosemary leaves, finely
   chopped
2 x 400g tins chopped tomatoes
15 fresh basil leaves, plus extra to garnish
80g freshly grated Grana Padano cheese
Chilli oil for garnish

For the béchamel sauce
50g salted butter
50g plain flour
500ml full-fat milk, cold
fresh nutmeg

1. Cook the pasta in a large saucepan of salted boiling water for about 5 minutes, drain, then place the shells, inverted, on a clean tea towel to cool.

2. For the béchamel sauce, melt the butter in a medium saucepan over a medium heat. Stir in the flour and cook for 1 minute until it becomes light brown in colour. Gradually whisk in the cold milk, reduce the heat and cook for 10 minutes, whisking constantly. Once thickened, grate over the nutmeg. Season with salt and pepper and set aside to slightly cool.

3. To prepare the meat sauce, melt the butter with the oil in a large frying pan and fry the onion for 2 minutes until softened, stirring occasionally. Add in the minced beef with the rosemary and cook, stirring continuously, until the meat has begun to crumble. Add a pinch of salt and pepper and cook for 15 minutes until the meat has browned. Set aside to cool. Once the meat has cooled down, pour half of the béchamel sauce in the pan and mix all together. Set aside.

4. Preheat the oven to 190°C/gas mark 5. Pour the chopped tomatoes into a small saucepan and bring to the boil. Lower the heat, add in the basil and season with salt and pepper. Cook for 8 minutes, stirring occasionally.

5. Spread the tomato sauce over the bottom of a 35 x 20cm ceramic dish; this will prevent the conchiglioni shells from sticking. Fill the shells with the meat mixture and gently place in the ceramic dish, making sure they aren't too close together. Drizzle the remaining béchamel over each filled shell.

6. Cover the dish with foil and bake in the middle of the oven for 15 minutes. Remove the foil, sprinkle with the Grana Padano and continue to cook for a further 5 minutes.

7. Allow the pasta to rest out of the oven for 3 minutes before serving it. Spoon some of the tomato sauce in the centre of a serving plate and arrange six filled pasta shells on top. Scatter over a few basil leaves and drizzle some chilli oil on top.

Pappardelle with sausages and leeks / PAPPARDELLE CON SALSICCE

My inspiration for this recipe came from my visit to the Chianti area. I tried a dish very similar to this and just had to create my own version. Their sauce was slightly thicker, so I'm sure they used mascarpone instead of double cream (which I've also tried and works well) but to me, this is the best way to serve this dish. If you are struggling to find Italian sausages, ask your butcher – you are looking for a high percentage of pork meat with herbs.

Serves 4

400g Italian sausages with herbs
50g salted butter
4 tablespoons olive oil
1 large leek, cut in half lengthwise and sliced into ½cm pieces
1 tablespoon fresh thyme leaves
200g fresh porcini mushrooms or chestnut mushrooms, cleaned and sliced
Salt and pepper to taste
100ml dry white wine
200ml double cream
500g dried pappardelle
3 tablespoons chopped fresh flat leaf parsley

1. Remove the meat from the sausages, place in a bowl and set aside. Over a medium heat, melt the butter with the oil in a large frying pan and fry the sausage meat and the leek for 10 minutes, stirring occasionally, until the meat has crumbled and browned all over. Add the thyme leaves and mushrooms, season with salt and pepper and continue to cook for 5 minutes. Pour in the wine and cook for a further minute. Pour in the cream, mix everything together and cook for 2 minutes on a low heat. Set aside away from the heat.

2. Meanwhile, cook the pasta in a large saucepan of salted boiling water until al dente. Stir occasionally to prevent it sticking. For the perfect al dente bite, cook the pasta 1 minute less than instructed on the packet. Drain and tip back into the same saucepan. Set the pan over a medium heat and pour over the creamy sausage sauce and the parsley. Mix everything together for 20 seconds to allow the flavours to combine beautifully and the sauce to stick to the pasta.

3. Check for seasoning one more time and serve immediately.

Potato and roasted pumpkin gnocchi / GNOCCHI DI ZUCCA

Gnocchi is a firm favourite of the ladies in my life – my wife and my daughter Mia. Rather than just preparing the traditional plain gnocchi with a tomato-and-cheese-based sauce all the time, I wanted to try and create gnocchi that had so much flavour in their own right that a sauce wasn't even needed. This is what I came up with. I have also tried replacing the pumpkin with butternut squash, which works just as well.

Serves 4

800g floury potatoes
Salt and white pepper to taste
500g pumpkin, cut into 3cm cubes
Extra virgin olive oil
½ teaspoon dried chilli flakes
1 tablespoon fresh rosemary leaves, finely chopped
2 large eggs, beaten
200g plain flour, plus extra for dusting
80g freshly grated Pecorino cheese to serve

1. Preheat the oven to 190°C/gas mark 5. Place the potatoes, skin on, in a large saucepan with 1 tablespoon of salt. Cover with water and bring to the boil. Boil for 30 minutes until softened and then, when cooked, drain, peel and put them through a ricer while still warm. Set aside.

2. Put the pumpkin cubes in a large baking tray and drizzle over a little oil to coat lightly. Sprinkle over the chilli flakes, rosemary leaves and season with salt. Mix everything together and roast in the oven for 30 minutes until tender and softened. Put the roasted pumpkin through a potato ricer and add to the potatoes, stirring well to combine.

3. Place the mixture on a clean surface and make a well in the centre. Add the eggs and season with salt and pepper. Gently knead the mixture with your hands. Add the flour a little at a time and work quickly, as the longer the dough is worked, the heavier the gnocchi become. Lightly dust a work surface with flour and shape the dough into several long rolls about 1.5cm in diameter. Cut each roll into 1.5cm pieces and set aside ready to be cooked.

4. Bring a large pan with salted water to the boil. Gently lower half of the gnocchi into the water, and cook, stirring gently, until they rise to the surface – about 2 minutes. Remove with a slotted spoon, drain and transfer to a large, warm serving plate. Repeat until all the gnocchi are cooked.

5. Serve drizzled with olive oil and sprinkled with Pecorino and a little white pepper.

Linguine with mussels and black pepper / LINGUINE ALLE COZZE E PEPE NERO

I must admit, if I'm ordering mussels on their own, I love to have them simply cooked just in white wine, but when it comes to creating a pasta sauce, for me, this is the only way to serve them. They are still allowed to take the star spot; however, the semi-dried tomatoes give them that touch of fresh tomato taste which really complements all the other flavours. A little tip; once you have drained the mussels and caught the broth in a separate bowl, just check there are no pieces of broken shell still in the pan before frying the
semi-dried tomatoes.

Serves 4

800g mussels
150ml dry white wine
5 tablespoons extra virgin olive oil
150g semi-dried tomatoes in oil, oil reserved
2 garlic cloves, peeled and finely sliced
Salt and black pepper to taste
500g dried linguine

1. Wash the mussels under cold water and discard any broken ones or any that do not close when tapped firmly. Place the mussels in a large saucepan, pour over the wine and cover with a lid. Cook over a medium heat for 5 minutes, until they have opened. Remove and discard any that remain closed and any empty shells. Tip into a colander placed over a bowl to catch the cooking liquor. Set both aside.

2. Pour the olive oil and the oil from the semi-dried tomatoes in the saucepan you cooked the mussels in. Over a medium heat, fry the garlic until it begins to sizzle. Add in the tomatoes and pour in the reserved cooking liquor from the mussels. Cook for 2 minutes and season with salt and lots of black pepper – and when I say lots of black pepper I mean at least ½ teaspoon full.

3. Meanwhile, cook the pasta in a large saucepan of salted boiling water until al dente. Stir occasionally to prevent it sticking. For the perfect al dente bite, cook the pasta 1 minute less than instructed on the packet. Drain and tip back into the same saucepan. Set the pan on a medium heat, pour over the sauce with the mussels and stir everything together for 10 seconds, allowing the flavours to combine and the sauce to stick to the pasta.

4. Serve immediately – please do not be tempted to serve it with grated cheese on top!

Pasta with sweet red onions, chilli and fillet steak / PENNETTE CON CIPOLLE ROSSE E MANZO

Chunky meat pasta sauces are very popular in the north of Italy and are absolutely delicious, so I was always going to include one in this chapter. I must make a confession, though; this particular recipe came about as a leftover concoction. I made a meat stew the night before for my family and the next night I came in late and needed to prepare something quickly as I was starving. I got the meat leftovers, poured them over some pasta – and here we are. You can use red wine if you prefer, but the white wine makes the sauce a lighter colour which, on this occasion, I prefer.

Serves 4

2 tablespoons salted butter
6 tablespoons olive oil
2 large red onions, peeled and finely sliced
1 large white onion, peeled and finely sliced
1 large carrot, peeled and grated
1 tablespoon fresh thyme leaves
350g beef fillet, cut into 1cm cubes
1 red chilli, deseeded and finely sliced
100ml white wine
400ml vegetable stock, made with stock cubes
Salt and black pepper to taste
500g dried pennette (slightly thinner than penne)

1. Melt the butter with the oil in a large saucepan over a medium heat and fry the onions, carrot and thyme for 10 minutes. Season with a little salt and stir occasionally with a wooden spoon. Add in the beef and chilli and continue to cook for 3 minutes, stirring frequently, until the meat has browned all over. Pour in the wine and cook for 2 minutes to allow the alcohol to evaporate. Pour in the stock, lower the heat, half-cover the pan with a lid and simmer for 40 minutes, stirring every 10 minutes.

2. Remove the lid and continue to cook for a further 10 minutes, allowing the sauce to thicken slightly. Season with salt and set aside.

3. Meanwhile, cook the pasta in a large saucepan of salted boiling water until al dente. Stir occasionally to prevent it sticking. For the perfect al dente bite, cook the pasta 1 minute less than instructed on the packet. Drain and tip back into the same saucepan. Set the pan over a low heat, pour over the onion and meat sauce and stir everything together for 20 seconds, allowing the flavours to combine and the sauce to stick to the pasta.

4. Serve immediately in warm pasta plates with a good bottle of Italian red wine.

Spaghetti with king prawns and tuna / SPAGHETTI AI GAMBERONI E TONNO

For those of you who love fish, this one is for you. The saltiness of the anchovies, together with the sweet prawns and the taste of the tuna in oil, is a match made in heaven. This is such a quick and easy recipe to put together – and talk about omega 3 intake! It is perfect for those keep-fit, health-conscious people who are looking for carbs after a workout but want the protein and minerals in abundance too.

Serves 4

12 fresh king prawns
10 tablespoons extra virgin olive oil
2 garlic cloves, peeled and finely sliced
150g Taggiasca pitted olives, drained and cut in half
4 anchovy fillets in oil, drained and chopped
½ teaspoon dried chilli flakes
1 x 400g tin cherry tomatoes
1 x 200g tin tuna in oil, drained and flaked
2 tablespoons chopped fresh flat leaf parsley
Salt to taste
500g dried spaghetti

1. Remove and discard the shell, heads and tails from the prawns. With a knife, make a cut along the back of each prawn and remove and discard the central vein. Cut in half lengthways and set aside.

2. Pour the oil in a large frying pan over a medium heat and start to fry the garlic, olives and anchovies for 1 minute. Stir with a wooden spoon. Add in the prawns with the chilli and continue to cook for a further 2 minutes. Pour in the tinned cherry tomatoes and cook for 5 minutes, stirring occasionally. Scatter the tuna and the parsley over the sauce, season with a little salt and stir all together for an extra minute. Set aside.

3. Meanwhile, cook the pasta in a large saucepan of salted boiling water until al dente. Stir occasionally to prevent it sticking. For the perfect al dente bite, cook the pasta 1 minute less than instructed on the packet. Drain and tip back into the same saucepan. Set the pan over a low heat, pour over the sauce and stir everything together for 10 seconds, allowing the flavours to combine and the sauce to stick to the pasta.

4. Serve immediately with a cold Italian beer – please do not be tempted to serve it with grated cheese on top!

Pasta with pesto, green beans and potatoes / PASTA CON PESTO GENOVESE, FAGIOLINI E PATATE

Originating from Genoa in Liguria, pesto is the godfather of sauces in northern Italy, where it will always be found on the menu. Its simple ingredients combine with pasta to make a wonderful, fresh-tasting dish which is much lighter in flavour and texture than the creamy, heavier ones on offer. I love pesto and I really urge you to try to make your own – many people say they don't like pesto sauce until they have tried a fresh, home-made one. You can replace the Pecorino with Parmesan, if you prefer.

Serves 4

50g basil, leaves only
10g rocket leaves
Salt and freshly ground pepper
1 large garlic clove
100–125ml extra virgin olive oil
50g pine nuts
10g walnuts
40g finely grated Pecorino cheese
1 large potato, peeled and cut into 1cm cubes
500g of your favourite dried short pasta (I'm using Trofie)
100g green beans, cut into 2cm lengths

1. Make the pesto in a large mortar and pestle or food processor. Place the basil and rocket leaves into the mortar then sprinkle in a pinch of salt and add the garlic. Add a dash of extra virgin olive oil then use the pestle to work everything into a paste. Once the leaves have broken down a little and the garlic is in small pieces, add the pine nuts and walnuts and start to grind them into a paste. Once you have a smoothish paste (you don't want it completely smooth), add a good amount of black pepper and the Pecorino cheese. Pour in the remaining extra virgin olive oil and check the seasoning.

2. Bring a large pan of salted water to the boil, add the potato cubes and cook for 4–6 minutes until tender. Using a slotted spoon, scoop out the potato chunks and transfer to a plate to cool slightly.

3. Add the pasta to the potato cooking water and cook according to the packet instruction, but reducing the time by 1 minute. About 2 minutes before the end of the cooking time, add the green beans.

4 Place the pesto in a large bowl, then, once the pasta and beans are cooked, drain them, reserving some of the cooking water. Tip the pasta and beans into the pesto, along with the potatoes and gently mix everything together to coat. Use a little of the cooking water to loosen the sauce, if necessary. Check the seasoning again, then serve.

Baked pasta with aubergines, red onions and Parmesan /

TORTIGLIONI ALLA PARMIGIANA

Full of vitamins, minerals and dietary fibre and with the potential to lower cholesterol and help manage weight, aubergines are a great choice for salads, stews and pasta sauces, yet hardly anyone ever uses them. They are fantastic fruits (no, I'm not going crazy – it's like the tomato) that offer so much taste and yet are incredibly good for you. This is a really delicious pasta bake that offers you all that you are expecting and more. You can add a few chilli flakes to the sauce if you like an extra kick.

Serves 6

150ml olive oil
2 large aubergines, cut into strips 1cm wide
Salt and black pepper to taste
2 large red onions, peeled and finely sliced
3 x 400g tins chopped tomatoes
15 fresh basil leaves
500g dried tortiglioni
80g freshly grated Parmesan cheese

1. Heat the olive oil in a large frying pan, add the aubergines and fry for 8 minutes until golden brown, stirring occasionally. Using a slotted spoon, remove the aubergines from the pan and drain on kitchen paper. Sprinkle with a little salt.

2. Using the same pan, fry the onions for 8 minutes, stirring occasionally. Add in the tomatoes with the basil, stir everything together and simmer on a medium heat for 15 minutes. Stir occasionally. Stir in the aubergines and continue to cook for a further 2 minutes. Season with salt and pepper and set aside.

3. Meanwhile, cook the pasta in a large saucepan of salted boiling water until al dente. Stir occasionally to prevent it sticking. For the perfect al dente bite, cook the pasta 1 minute less than instructed on the packet. Drain and tip back into the saucepan. Set the pan over a low heat, pour over the aubergine sauce and half of the Parmesan. Stir everything together for 30 seconds, allowing all the flavours to combine.

4. Heat the grill to high. Transfer the pasta and sauce to a large ovenproof dish and sprinkle the top with the remaining Parmesan. Place under the grill for 10 minutes until the top gets bubbly and crispy. Remove and leave to rest for 5 minutes before cutting into portions. *Buon appetito!*

RICE & RISOTTO

If you are looking for a staple food that more than half the world's population consumes, rice comes top of the list. Rice wasn't actually seen as a food source in Italy until the fifteenth century, when cultivation spread to the north of the country where the fertile swampy plains provided perfect growing conditions.

The actual origins of rice being used to create risotto are not recorded, but it is definitely a very popular option throughout northern Italy. Like many of today's great Italian dishes, risotto used to be known as a peasant dish, which is probably why it is such a great comfort food. However, don't be fooled by this easy concept, as risotto can be dressed up to be as elegant and special as the pricier top selections on any menu.

Rice is grown extensively in Emilia-Romagna, Lombardy and Veneto, and Italy is now the biggest producer of rice in Europe. Italians divide rice into four categories: grain length, form/shape, cooking time and flavour (some are very aromatic), but to be honest there are so many varieties available now that it would be difficult to list them all.

Italy's most famous export, though, is the *fantastico* Arborio risotto rice. Risotto rice differs from other rice in that the starch content is much higher, which is what gives it the creamy texture when cooked. Arborio rice has been developed over the years to be able to absorb liquid when cooked, yet have a firm bite and a creamy texture.

Preparation for making a risotto dish starts slowly, usually with frying off onions and toasting the rice, adding in some wine and then slowly adding in simmering chicken, vegetable or fish broth. In northern Italy, a vegetable risotto is most popularly served during spring, with more hearty, meatier options on offer in winter.

I can eat risotto all year round as a starter or a main meal, and either way it will be received with excitement. Rice also makes a fantastic alternative to potatoes in other dishes, and, unlike risotto, where you are stuck to the pan for twenty minutes constantly stirring, with rice you can just put it in boiling water and leave it to fluff up and be fabulous. It is an amazing ingredient that can transform any meal. Please have a go – it's not as scary as you think and, once mastered, the options available are a culinary delight.

Simple saffron risotto / RISOTTO ALLO ZAFFERANO

What I love about this risotto is its versatility. You can make it for your main meal or as an accompaniment to any meat or fish. This simple risotto has a touch of elegance, with a slight bitter-honey taste running through it and the saffron lending it a lovely yellow colour. This small spice is not cheap, but it is so special in so many ways – just a pinch of saffron adds a little bit of wow to even the most humble dish.

Serves 4

½ teaspoon saffron strands
1.3 litres hot vegetable stock, made with stock cubes
1 large onion, peeled and finely chopped
6 tablespoons olive oil
400g Arborio or Carnaroli rice
150ml white wine
100g salted butter
80g Parmesan cheese, freshly grated
Salt and white pepper to taste

1. Mix the saffron with 4 tablespoons of hot stock in a small bowl and set aside.

2. In a large, heavy based saucepan, fry the onion in the oil for 3 minutes until soft but not browned, stirring. Add in the rice and fry for 3 minutes on a medium heat, allowing the rice to toast into the hot oil. Stir continuously with a wooden spoon. Pour the wine over the rice and continue to cook for a further minute to allow the alcohol to evaporate.

3. Stir in the saffron mixture then add a couple of ladles of stock and bring to a simmer. Continue to cook and stir until all the stock is absorbed. At this point please stay with the saucepan because you need to keep stirring with a wooden spoon. Pour in the rest of the stock, a little at a time, cooking until each addition is absorbed. It is ready when all the liquid has been absorbed and the rice is cooked but still has a slight bite. This will take 15–17 minutes, you may not need all the stock.

4. Once the rice is cooked, take the pan off the heat and add in the butter with the Parmesan. At this point stir everything together for 30 seconds to allow the risotto to become creamy. Season with salt and pepper and serve immediately.

Risotto with red radicchio and Italian sausages / RISOTTO AL RADICCHIO

ROSSO E SALSICCIA

I can't think of anything better than sitting and eating a plate of risotto while admiring the view of the winding canals of Venice. This risotto has all the colours of Italy – green peas, creamy white rice and the sharp red of a favourite regional leaf vegetable, radicchio.

Serves 4

2 tablespoons olive oil, plus extra for drizzling
25g butter
4 sausages, skins removed
1 onion, very finely chopped
2 celery sticks, very finely chopped
400g Arborio or Carnaroli rice
100ml white wine
1.3 litres hot vegetable or chicken stock
150g frozen peas, defrosted
¼ head of radicchio, finely sliced
100g butter
80g Parmesan cheese, finely grated
Salt and freshly ground black pepper

1. Heat the olive oil and butter in a large heavy based frying pan on a high heat. When hot, add the sausage meat and fry, using a wooden spoon to break up the meat into small pieces. Fry until golden brown, then transfer to a plate lined with kitchen paper using a slotted spoon. Keep warm.

2. In the same pan, cook the onion and celery for 2 minutes, then add the rice and fry for 3 minutes on a medium heat, allowing the rice to toast into the hot oil. Stir continuously with a wooden spoon. Pour the wine over the rice and continue to cook for a further minute to allow the alcohol to evaporate.

3. Add a couple of ladles of stock and bring to a simmer. Continue to cook and stir until all the stock is absorbed. At this point please stay with the saucepan because you need to keep stirring with a wooden spoon. Pour in the rest of the stock, except one ladleful, a little at a time, cooking until each addition is absorbed. It is ready when all the liquid has been absorbed and the rice is cooked but still has a slight bite. This will take 15–17 minutes (you may not need all the stock).

4. When the rice is just cooked, add the peas and radicchio. Add a final ladle of stock, stir, then remove from the heat and stir in the butter and Parmesan. Once the butter has melted, add three-quarters of the cooked and crumbled sausage meat. Season to taste.

5. Serve in warm bowls topped with the rest of the cooked sausage, a drizzle of olive oil and a little freshly ground black pepper.

Baked risotto with aubergine, basil and mozzarella / RISOTTO AL
FORNO CON MELANZANE, BASILICO E MOZZARELLA

This has to be the ultimate vegetarian meal. It is so full of flavour, so good for you and so tasty. It is a bit time-consuming to prepare but the beauty of it is that you can do it in the afternoon, relax, and then just pop it in the oven for 30 minutes when ready. (If you do go for this option, make sure you take it out of the fridge 20 minutes beforehand.) One time I made this I only had two aubergines, so I did one layer of aubergines and one of courgettes, which also worked really well.

Serves 4

2 x 125g packs mozzarella (not buffalo mozzarella)
1 x 700ml bottle of passata (sieved tomatoes)
1 x 400g tin chopped tomatoes
10 fresh basil leaves
Salt and black pepper to taste
Sunflower or vegetable oil for frying
3 large aubergines, cut into ½cm slices
100g plain flour
1 quantity of saffron risotto (page 134)
50g salted butter for greasing
120g Parmesan cheese, freshly grated

1. Preheat the oven to 190°C/gas mark 5. Grease an ovenproof dish measuring 30 x 22cm and 8cm deep. Drain the mozzarella balls and cut each into 8 slices. Set aside.

2. Pour the passata and chopped tomatoes into a bowl with the basil leaves, season with salt and pepper, mix and set aside.

3. Pour 2cm of oil into a large frying pan over a medium heat. Coat the aubergine slices in the flour, tapping off any excess, then fry in batches until golden and brown on both sides. Carefully remove with a slotted spoon and drain on kitchen paper to absorb any excess oil. Repeat until all the aubergine is cooked. Set aside.

4. Pour half of the tomato sauce into the ovenproof dish and scatter over one-third of the mozzarella slices. Cover with half the aubergine slices. Spread all the saffron risotto over, and top with the remaining aubergine slices. Scatter over another third of mozzarella slices and then add the remaining tomato sauce. Scatter over the remaining mozzarella and finish with the Parmesan. Season with salt and pepper. Bake in the middle of the oven for 25 minutes until cooked through and the cheese is golden and bubbling.

5. Remove from the oven and let it rest for about 5 minutes, to make it easier to cut. Serve hot or at room temperature.

Risotto with fresh crab, lemon and parsley / RISOTTO CON GRANCHIO, LIMONE E PREZZEMOLO

Crab is such a meaty shellfish and I love cooking with it. I have chosen to use it here instead of lobster mainly because it is the cheaper option. Both give a similar taste and texture to this dish, so why spend more? I have kept this risotto simple, using only butter and fish stock to cook with, to allow the natural flavours of the sea to take centrestage. Please, whatever you do, don't buy crab sticks – it has to be the real thing for you to get the right taste experience. You could also use cooked prawns for this risotto.

Serves 4

1 large onion, peeled and finely chopped
6 tablespoons olive oil
400g Arborio or Carnaroli rice
150ml white wine
1.3 litres hot fish stock, made with stock cubes
60g salted butter
4 tablespoons chopped fresh flat leaf parsley
Juice of ½ lemon
200g fresh white crab meat
Salt and black pepper to taste

1. In a large heavy-based saucepan, fry the onion in the oil for 3 minutes until soft but not browned, stirring occasionally. Add in the rice and fry for 3 minutes on a medium heat to allow the rice to toast into the hot oil. Stir continuously with a wooden spoon. Pour the wine over the rice and continue to cook for a further minute to allow the alcohol to evaporate.

2. Add a couple of ladles of stock and bring to a simmer. Continue to cook and stir until all the stock is absorbed. At this point please stay with the saucepan because you need to keep stirring with a wooden spoon. Pour in the rest of the stock, a little at a time, cooking until each addition is absorbed. It is ready when all the liquid has been absorbed and the rice is cooked but still has a slight bite. This will take 15–17 minutes (you may not need all the stock).

3. Once the rice is cooked, take the pan off the heat and add in the butter, parsley, lemon juice and crab meat.

4. Stir everything together for 30 seconds to allow the risotto to become creamy and all the ingredients to combine. Season with salt and pepper and serve immediately without any kind of cheese on top, otherwise you will ruin the fresh flavours of the crab.

Four-cheese risotto with fresh chives / RISOTTO AI QUATTRO FORMAGGI

You would think that the high cheese content here might leave your stomach feeling really heavy, but somehow it doesn't. It might be because I've only used small amounts of various different cheeses – most of which are produced in the north – so although you get the strong flavours coming through and you create a really creamy risotto, it doesn't leave you with that stuffed, uncomfortable feeling – unless, of course, you make this recipe for four and only eat it between two. But then that's your fault rather than my recipe! I must admit it's hard to resist once you've tried it, though.

Serves 4

1 large onion, peeled and finely chopped
6 tablespoons olive oil
400g Arborio or Carnaroli rice
150ml white wine
1.3 litres hot vegetable stock, made with
   stock cubes
100g salted butter
4 tablespoons finely chopped fresh chives
30g Gorgonzola, cut into small cubes
30g Fontina, cut into small cubes
30g Provolone piccante, cut into small cubes
50g Pecorino cheese, freshly grated
Salt and white pepper to taste

1. In a large heavy-based saucepan, fry the onion in the oil for 3 minutes until soft but not browned, stirring occasionally. Add in the rice and fry for 3 minutes on a medium heat to allow the rice to toast in the hot oil. Stir continuously with a wooden spoon. Pour the wine over the rice and continue to cook for a further minute to allow the alcohol to evaporate.

2. Add a couple of ladles of stock and bring to a simmer. Continue to cook and stir until all the stock is absorbed. At this point please stay with the saucepan because you need to keep stirring with a wooden spoon. Pour in the rest of the stock, a little at a time, cooking until each addition is absorbed. It is ready when all the liquid has been absorbed and the rice is cooked but still has a slight bite. This will take 15–17 minutes (you may not need all the stock).

3. Once the rice is cooked, take the pan off the heat and add in the butter, the chives and all the cheese. At this point, stir everything together for 30 seconds to allow the risotto to become creamy. Season with salt and pepper and serve immediately.

Seafood risotto / RISOTTO AI FRUTTI DI MARE

This delicious risotto is dedicated to my late father, Ciro. He absolutely loved seafood and I know he would have devoured this dish in seconds. I have also made this same meal using clams instead of mussels and both work really well. Unfortunately this is not a dish that can be reheated, but that's OK because I'm pretty sure there'll be none left over anyway.

Serves 4

150g fresh mussels
4 tablespoons olive oil
1 large red onion, peeled and finely chopped
½ teaspoon dried chilli flakes
350g Arborio or Carnaroli rice
150ml dry white wine
1.2 litres hot fish stock, made from stock cubes
150g fresh raw prawns, peeled, heads and tails removed
100g large scallops with the coral, cut in half
Zest of 1 unwaxed lemon
50g salted butter
15 cherry tomatoes, cut into quarters
4 tablespoons chopped fresh flat leaf parsley

1. Place the mussels in the sink and under cold running water, scrape off any grit. With your fingers, pull away the hairy beards that protrude from the shells. Using the back of a knife, tap any mussels that remain open, discarding any that refuse to close. Rinse again in cold water until there is no trace of sand and dirt. Set aside.

2. Heat the olive oil in a large saucepan and fry the onion and chilli on a medium heat for 3 minutes, stirring occasionally until soft. Add the rice and keep stirring for 3 minutes to allow it to toast in the oil. Pour in the wine and continue to cook for a further 2 minutes to allow the alcohol to evaporate, stirring occasionally.

3. Start to add the stock a little at a time and cook gently, stirring until the stock is absorbed. Continue adding the stock as each addition is absorbed. (If you need to, add more hot water to the stock.) Just before most of the stock has been absorbed (about 10 minutes), add in the prawns, scallops, mussels and lemon zest and continue to cook for a further 5 minutes until the prawns have turned pink and the rice is cooked but still has a slight bite.

4. When the risotto is ready, take the saucepan off the heat and add the butter with the cherry tomatoes. It is very important that you stir the butter into the rice for at least 30 seconds to create a smooth, creamy texture. Stir in the parsley and serve immediately.

Treviso-style risotto with radicchio and dry vermouth /

RISOTTO ALLA TREVISANA

I know this sounds kind of weird, but I think radicchio is an amazing-looking vegetable that we just don't use enough. The Treviso Tardivo variety is in season between November and April in Treviso and has a crunchy texture with a pleasant bitter taste. The bright red/purple splayed leaves just make it look so great and, of course, like lots of veg, it also offers a lot of goodness. It is apparently fantastic for treating insomnia and purifying the blood, but for me, it just gives the risotto an extra-special taste and texture that works beautifully. When you shop for this recipe buy a few more Treviso Tardivo radicchio and try them in your salad – yum!

Serves 4

100g salted butter, room temperature
4 tablespoons olive oil
1 large onion, peeled and finely chopped
1 tablespoon fresh rosemary leaves, finely
  chopped
400g Arborio or Carnaroli rice
150ml dry vermouth
500g Treviso Tardivo radicchio, cut into 3cm
  pieces
1.3 litres hot vegetable stock, made with
  stock cubes
80g Parmesan cheese, freshly grated
Salt and black pepper to taste

1. Melt half the butter with the oil in a large heavy based saucepan over a medium heat, then fry the onion and rosemary for 5 minutes until soft but not browned, stirring occasionally. Add in the rice and fry for 3 minutes allowing the rice to toast, stirring continuously. Pour the vermouth over the rice and continue to cook for a further minute to allow the alcohol to evaporate.

2. Add a couple of ladles of stock and bring to a simmer. Continue to cook and stir until all the stock is absorbed. At this point please stay with the saucepan because you need to keep stirring. Add in the radicchio pieces and pour in the rest of the stock, a little at the time, cooking until each addition is absorbed. It is ready when all the liquid has been absorbed and the rice is cooked but still has a slight bite. This takes 15–17 minutes (you may not need all the stock).

3. Once the rice is cooked, take the pan off the heat and add in the remaining butter with the Parmesan. Stir everything together for 20 seconds to allow the risotto to become creamy. The risotto should not be too thick – you want it to ooze. Season with salt and pepper and serve immediately. *Buon appetito!*

Traditional Venetian rice dish with pancetta and peas / RISI E BISI

Picture the scene... we have walked all around Venice, filming in many different locations and, finally, at the end of the day, we are sitting outside a café-style restaurant. All the crew are ordering salads or light meals as it's a hot evening and here I am ordering this dish – a heavy, creamy, thick, soup-like risotto. I was not disappointed and the others definitely had food envy. I had to bring this recipe home with me and put it in this book; it is an absolute winner and the kids love it. If you decide to serve this as a starter, make sure you only serve a very small bowl or your guests won't have room for the main!

Serves 4

60g salted butter
3 tablespoons olive oil
1 large onion, peeled and finely chopped
150g diced pancetta
500g frozen small peas
3 tablespoons chopped fresh flat leaf parsley
1.5 litres hot vegetable stock, made with stock
  cubes
400g Arborio or Carnaroli rice
50g Parmesan cheese, freshly grated
Extra virgin olive oil for drizzling
Salt and white pepper to taste

1. Melt 40g of the butter with the oil in a large saucepan and fry the onion with the pancetta for 5 minutes, stirring occasionally. Add in the peas with the parsley and two ladlefuls of hot stock. Simmer, with the lid off, for 15 minutes until the stock has evaporated.

2 Add in the rice and gently stir on a medium heat for 2 minutes. Pour in 500ml of stock and continue to cook, stirring occasionally. As soon as the water has been absorbed, add more stock a ladleful at a time. Continue to cook for 20 minutes until the risotto has a soupy consistency and the rice is cooked but still has a slight bite.

3. Remove the saucepan from the heat and stir in the remaining butter with the Parmesan. Cover the saucepan with a lid and leave to rest for 3 minutes. Serve in warm bowls with a little extra virgin olive oil drizzled on top.

Traditional Italian rice salad /

INSALATA DI RISO CLASSICA

Rice salads are, in general, a very popular choice all over Italy. We are more likely to have a cold rice salad to accompany a meat or fish dish than potatoes, often with a separate bowl of lettuce leaves or sliced tomatoes drizzled with olive oil. This rice salad, however, is a meal in itself and can be served just as is. It is perfect for a lunch stop or if you are out and about or to take to work. We never have a picnic without this salad in our hamper. Anything goes, really, and you can be as creative as you want – but, for me, this combination is perfect.

Serves 6

Salt and white pepper to taste
350g long grain or basmati rice
100g fresh or frozen peas
100g Taggiasca pitted olives, cut in half
100g pickled small gherkins, chopped into
  small pieces
1 yellow pepper, deseeded and chopped into
  small pieces
1 red pepper, deseeded and chopped into
  small pieces
1 x 200g tin tuna in oil, drained
3 tablespoons bought mayonnaise
4 tablespoons extra virgin olive oil
10 cherry tomatoes, cut into quarters
100g Parmesan cheese, shaved
6 hard-boiled eggs, peeled and cut into quarters

1. Half-fill a medium saucepan with water and add in 1 tablespoon of salt, then bring to the boil. Cook the rice for 10 minutes, stirring occasionally, then add in the peas and continue to boil for a further 5 minutes. Drain, then rinse under cold running water for 1 minute. Drain well again and tip into a large mixing bowl. (Depending on the quality of the rice, you may have to vary the cooking time.)

2. Add all the ingredients to the mixing bowl except for the Parmesan and the boiled eggs. Season with salt and pepper, mix well and cover with cling film. Leave to rest into the fridge for 2 hours, stirring every 30 minutes, to allow the flavours to combine.

3. Take the rice out of the fridge 20 minutes before serving. Divide among 6 serving plates, arrange the boiled eggs around it and scatter over the Parmesan shavings. *Buon appetito!*

Leek, Taleggio and pine kernel risotto / RISOTTO CON PORRI, TALEGGIO E PINOLI

Leeks make a fantastic alternative to onions, and yet many people only use them in soups. I got inspiration for this recipe while I was in Siena; I was served a bowl of leeks, cheese, nuts and sausages (which is also a great sauce for pasta) and I wanted to try and incorporate the same flavours in a risotto. I have left this as a vegetarian option, but by all means add in some cooked pancetta or sausage meat if you wish. I have tried this recipe using goat's cheese, which is also great, but if you do this, the recipe works better if it is kept meat-free.

Serves 4

100g salted butter
120ml olive oil
200g leeks, finely chopped
400g Arborio or Carnaroli rice
Leaves from 4 fresh thyme sprigs
150ml white wine
1.3 litres hot vegetable stock, made with stock cubes
60g pine kernels
200g Taleggio cheese, roughly chopped and rind removed
Salt and black pepper to taste

1. Melt half of the butter with the oil in a large heavy-based saucepan over a medium heat, then fry the leeks for 3 minutes until soft but not browned, stirring with a wooden spoon.

2. Add the rice with the thyme leaves and fry for 3 minutes, stirring continuously, to allow the rice to toast. Pour the wine over and continue to cook for a further minute to allow the alcohol to evaporate.

3. Add a couple of ladles of stock and bring to a simmer. Continue to cook and stir until all the stock is absorbed. At this point, please stay with the saucepan because you need to keep stirring as you pour in the rest of the stock, a little at a time, cooking until each addition is absorbed. It is ready when all the liquid has been absorbed and the rice is cooked but still has a slight bite. This will take 15–17 minutes (you may not need all the stock).

4. Take the pan off the heat and add in the pine kernels, the remaining butter and the Taleggio. Stir everything together for 30 seconds to allow the risotto to become creamy. Season with salt and pepper and serve immediately.

MEAT & GAME

The north of Italy is renowned for the quality of its meat, having excellent cattle breeds as well as excellent hogs. Consequently, veal, beef and pork – and, in some areas, rabbit and even horse – are the main meats of choice.

The method by which these meats are cooked ranges from slow braising and stewing to boiling and frying, and northern cooks tend to use much less tomato in their recipes – preferring to use wine or broth as the sauce, flavoured with chopped herbs. Boiled meats were not traditionally as popular as roasted meats in many Italian societies, but they have always been a huge favourite in the northern regions and will change doubtful minds once tried.

As I've mentioned already, the north of Italy is definitely a land of butter and lard, as opposed to the olive oil favoured by the south. Here the meat is cooked simply in butter and herbs, which really allows you to taste the natural flavours of the ingredients and appreciate a creamier texture. The preferred taste of creamy, meat-rich and

nutritious dishes is significantly enhanced by the wines produced by the fabulous vineyards you find in abundance in the north. You will always find a stewed meat or a veal or chicken in a cream and wine sauce on offer in nearly every restaurant. What I already knew about but was still amazed to experience were the variations in the cooking styles across the northern areas. Ragù, for example, tends to be less about tomatoes and more about the meat and aromatic herbs that flavour them, but Venetian ragù is made from the meat of the wild ducks that populate the lagoons and is perfumed with native bay leaf and fresh sage. Some such

dishes use duck stock, liver and giblets, while others get a deep flavour from duck legs and thighs and dry red wine. It's absolutely amazing that you can travel just over an hour away in a car and ask for the same dish and get something completely different. I have chosen a range of my favourites here and hope you enjoy them as much as I do.

Crispy chicken breast stuffed with mozzarella and pesto / PETTO DI POLLO RIPIENO CON MOZZARELLA E PESTO

Pesto originated in Genoa and is a firm favourite as a pasta sauce choice, but why stop there? It is also a fabulous option for stuffing white meat, as this one small ingredient holds so many flavours. Traditionally a good pesto consists of garlic, fresh basil leaves, Parmesan, pine nuts and olive oil, and for me this remains the superior version. Here pesto makes stuffed breaded chicken extra special; done like this, it really doesn't get any better. You can use Taleggio instead of mozzarella, if you prefer, and please, please make sure you use a good-quality pesto if shop-bought or, even better, make a fresh batch. You also may need to use more than one toothpick if you are using large chicken breasts.

Serves 6

4 large boneless and skinless chicken breasts
4 tablespoons shop-bought basil pesto, plus
  1 tablespoon extra to serve
1 x 125g pack mozzarella, cut into 4 sticks
4 sun-dried tomatoes in oil, drained
60g plain flour
180g breadcrumbs
Salt and black pepper to taste
2 eggs, beaten
100ml vegetable or sunflower oil
olive oil to serve

1. Preheat the oven to 210°C/gas mark 7. With the help of a long sharp knife, make a hole in the thicker end of each chicken breast. Push the knife inside towards the pointed end of the fillet and slide it back and forth to cut a long pocket inside the breast, but don't cut it open completely. Push a tablespoon of pesto, one mozzarella stick and one sun-dried tomato into each pocket, securing with one or two toothpicks at the fat end.

2. Place the flour and breadcrumbs on two separate plates. Season the chicken breasts with salt and pepper then dip each breast first in flour, then in the eggs and finally in the breadcrumbs. Set aside.

3. Pour the oil into a large frying pan and, once hot, fry the stuffed chicken breasts for 2 minutes on each side until the crumbs are crisp and browned. Transfer to a baking tray and cook in the oven for 15 minutes or until the chicken is cooked through.

4. Loosen 1 tablespoon of pesto with a little olive oil and drizzle it over the chicken. Serve hot with my favourite potatoes (see page 203) and a crispy salad. *Buon appetito!*

Chicken in balsamic vinegar with asparagus and cherry tomato salad / POLLO ALL'ACETO
BALSAMICO CON INSALATA DI POMODORI E ASPARAGI

Balsamic vinegar is a true flavour of northern Italy. The real thing is made in Modena, in Emilia-Romagna, and the bottle will be labelled *'tradizionale'* or DOC. This is the best, but it is also the most expensive. Try to get the best you can afford for this recipe – you don't need much and it really does make a difference to the dish. Do not buy the really cheap versions – it is never a good idea!

Serves 4

1 tablespoon olive oil
4 chicken thighs, bone in and skin on
4 chicken drumsticks, bone in and skin on
200g smoked pancetta, diced
3 garlic cloves, sliced
A few fresh thyme sprigs
150ml white wine
300ml chicken or vegetable stock
3 tablespoons balsamic vinegar

For the salad
200g fine asparagus tips, cut in half lengthways
200g cherry tomatoes, quartered
A few fresh flat leaf parsley leaves
Juice of 1 lemon
3 tablespoons extra virgin olive oil

1. Heat the oil in a large sauté pan with a lid or a casserole dish. Put the chicken pieces in the pan skin-side down and fry for 5–7 minutes until the skin is golden brown and really crispy. Season with salt and pepper. Turn the chicken over, season the skin and add the pancetta. Cook for a minute before adding the garlic and thyme. The pancetta should be crispy when done.

2. Deglaze the pan with the white wine, scraping up all the caramelized bits from the bottom of the pan. Allow the alcohol to bubble for a minute, then add the stock. Cover the pan and simmer gently for 1 hour, adding more stock if the contents of the pan become dry.

3. While the chicken is cooking, place the asparagus, tomatoes, parsley leaves, lemon juice and extra virgin olive oil in a large bowl. Season with salt and pepper then toss everything together. Leave to stand for 20 minutes.

4. When the chicken is cooked, remove it from the heat – the sauce should have reduced and thickened. Stir in the balsamic vinegar, return the pan to the heat for 1 minute to warm the sauce, then serve the chicken and sauce with the asparagus salad.

Simple Italian-style roast chicken with thyme and garlic /

POLLO ARROSTO SEMPLICE

A simple roast chicken is always a winner in my house, and considering it's less than five minutes of preparation time and then just putting it in the oven, it has to be the easiest meal in the world. I've obviously put a northern-Italian twist on this by adding a couple of simple tasty ingredients to enhance the natural flavours and, personally, I like to lay some peeled potatoes or other veg around the chicken so they take on the flavours too.

Serves 6

2 whole chickens (about 1.2kg each)
60g salted butter, at room temperature
1 small bunch of fresh thyme
20 garlic cloves
1 unwaxed lemon, sliced, with the skin on
Olive oil
2 tablespoons runny honey
Salt and black pepper to taste
150ml vegetable stock, made with stock cubes

1. Preheat the oven to 210°C/gas mark 7. Place the chickens in a large roasting tin and rub them all over with the butter. Place half the thyme inside the cavities with the garlic and lemon slices. Scatter the remaining thyme around the chickens and drizzle a little oil and honey over the birds. Season with salt and pepper, pour in the stock and cover the whole tray with foil. Roast in the oven for 1 hour.

2. Remove the foil from the tray and continue to roast for a further 15 minutes to allow the chickens to colour beautifully. To make sure the chicken is cooked, stick the tip of a knife into the thickest part of the thigh; if the juices run clear, it's ready. If the juices are still pink, leave to cook for another 15 minutes.

3 Transfer the chickens to a warm serving plate and leave to rest for 5 minutes before carving to allow the meat to become juicy and tender. Enjoy with a large amount of potatoes and your favourite vegetables on the side.

Venetian-style calf's liver in white wine and sage sauce /
FEGATO ALLA VENEZIANA

I absolutely love calf's liver – if cooked well, it is the most delicious meat you could have. It is also very nutritious. Not only does it contain high levels of minerals and vitamins, but it is also an amazing source of protein, and will help improve your cardiovascular health and aid immune function. But to me all this is just a bonus, because the taste is what it's all about. I have kept this Venetian recipe simple as I wanted you to taste the natural flavours of the liver and I've suggested serving it with my saffron risotto, although many Italians would serve it with polenta and most people here would choose mash.

Serves 4

1kg calf's liver
8 tablespoons extra virgin olive oil
2 large white onions, peeled and finely sliced
Salt and freshly ground black pepper to taste
16 fresh sage leaves
60ml dry white wine
60g salted butter

1. Trim and clean the liver and slice it very thinly. Cut each slice into thin triangles and set aside.

2. Pour 4 tablespoons of oil in a large frying pan and fry the onions with a pinch of salt on a very low heat for 30 minutes, stirring regularly with a wooden spoon. The onions should not burn but should become translucent and light brown in colour. Mix in a pinch of pepper and set aside away from the heat.

3. Heat the remaining oil in a large frying pan over a medium heat, add in the sage leaves with the liver and cook for 1 minute on each side. Add a pinch of salt and the onions to the liver and cook for a further 30 seconds. Pour in the wine, turn up the heat and allow to bubble for 1 minute. Add in the butter and continue to cook for a further minute.

4. Season with salt and pepper and serve immediately with your favourite salad or with delicious saffron risotto (see page 134).

Roasted pheasant in red wine sauce / FAGIANO AL VINO ROSSO

Game is very popular in northern Italy because its flat lowlands and lagoons provide a perfect habitat for the birds. The north is also home to my favourite vegetable of all time, and one that isn't used that much here – fennel – so I wanted to create a recipe that would combine the two. Any meat cooked in wine allows the flavour to wow you and results in lovely buttery textures, but adding the fennel gives you that mild anise flavour which really complements this creamy dish. If you prefer, quail also works well.

Serves 4

2 hen pheasants
Salt and freshly ground black pepper to taste
4 fresh rosemary sprigs
2 garlic cloves, peeled
60g salted butter
3 tablespoons olive oil
1 celery head, outer stalks removed, hearts
   quartered lengthways
2 large fennel bulbs, trimmed and quartered
250g diced smoked pancetta
750ml Italian rich red wine
100g mascarpone cheese

1. Preheat the oven to 160°C/gas mark 3. Season the cavity of each pheasant with salt and pepper. Push into each cavity two sprigs of rosemary and one garlic clove.

2. Melt the butter and oil in an ovenproof casserole dish over a high heat. Brown the pheasants on all sides, transfer to a bowl and keep warm. Add the celery, fennel and pancetta to the casserole dish and fry for 10 minutes. Season with salt and pepper and stir occasionally with a wooden spoon. Pour in two-thirds of the wine and bring to a simmer. Transfer the pheasants to the casserole dish, breast side down. Cover the dish with a lid and cook in the oven for 30 minutes. Turn the birds over, cover again and continue to cook for a further 30 minutes.

3. Remove the pheasants from the dish and set aside in a warm place. Pour the remaining wine into the dish and bring to the boil. Lower the heat to medium and simmer to reduce to a syrupy consistency. Stir occasionally with a wooden spoon. Remove the celery and fennel with a slotted spoon and place on a warm serving dish. Add the mascarpone to the pan and stir on a low heat for 1 minute until you create a thick sauce.

4. Cut the pheasants in half, place on top of the vegetables and pour over the rich sauce to serve.

Veal shanks with Parma ham and white wine / OSSOBUCO ALLA MILANESE

This has to be one of my favourite meat dishes of all time. The meat is truly like butter and your guests will really feel like you have gone way beyond the call of duty when you serve this. Remember to place a teaspoon next to your knife and fork to remind you to spoon out the marrow in the bone – to me that's the best part. You can replace the Parma ham with pancetta if you prefer. Another tip is to prepare a light starter for a dinner party if this is your main meal, as this really has to be the star of the show and you don't want your guests too full before they get to it.

Serves 6

8 tablespoons olive oil
150g Parma ham, diced into ½cm cubes
Plain flour for dusting
Salt and black pepper to taste
1.5kg veal shin on the bone, cut into 6 pieces
  each about 6cm thick
1 large red onion, peeled and finely chopped
2 large celery sticks, finely chopped
2 carrots, peeled and finely chopped
4 tablespoons fresh rosemary leaves plus a few
  sprigs for decoration
2 tablespoons tomato purée
150ml white wine
600ml hot beef stock

1. Preheat the oven to 170°C/gas mark 4. Pour the oil in a large frying pan and fry the Parma ham for 8 minutes until golden and crispy, stirring occasionally with a wooden spoon. Remove the ham with a slotted spoon and set aside, leaving the oil in the frying pan.

2. Put the flour on a plate, season generously with salt and pepper, and dip in the veal pieces to coat all over. Shake off any excess flour then place the veal in the frying pan in which you cooked the ham. Fry the meat for 5 minutes on each side until sealed and browned all over. Remove from the pan with a slotted spoon and set aside, leaving the oil in the frying pan.

3. Add the onion, celery and carrots to the frying pan and cook, stirring continuously, for 10 minutes until softened and beginning to brown. Add in the rosemary, cooked ham and tomato purée and mix together with a wooden spoon. Pour in the wine and simmer for 5 minutes to allow the alcohol to evaporate. Pour in the stock, stir, and cook for a further 5 minutes.

4. Spoon one-third of the sauce into a large casserole dish. Place the veal on top then pour over the remaining sauce, covering the meat as much as possible. Put the lid on and transfer to the oven for 1 hour. Remove the lid and cook for a further 30 minutes.

5. Serve immediately with saffron risotto (see page 134).

Rabbit in white wine, rosemary, olive and tomato sauce / CONIGLIO

ALLA CACCIATORE

Many people might be nervous about cooking rabbit, but actually, if you get your butcher to cut the meat into pieces, it's just like handling any other meat. The flavour of rabbit does give you a fantastic alternative to the traditional meat options. Northern Italians are huge fans of rabbit and in the past would have used wild animals, but nowadays most rabbits eaten in Italy are farmed – and to be honest these really are the best for cooking because they are tender and fatty, whereas the wild ones can sometimes be very tough. Give this dish a try – you won't be disappointed.

Serves 6

1 rabbit, cut into 12 pieces (ask your butcher to do this)
100g plain white flour
Salt and freshly ground black pepper to taste
150ml olive oil
3 carrots, peeled and finely chopped
3 celery sticks, finely chopped
2 tablespoons fresh rosemary leaves, finely chopped
1 large red onion, peeled and finely sliced
100ml white wine
2 x 400g tins chopped tomatoes
150g pitted Taggiasca black olives, drained and cut in half
5 tablespoons chopped fresh flat leaf parsley

1. Preheat the oven to 160°C/gas mark 3. Place the rabbit pieces in a large bowl with the flour and plenty of salt and pepper. Give it a good shake and transfer the rabbit to a plate. Heat the olive oil in a large frying pan and fry the rabbit pieces until browned on all sides. Remove with a slotted spoon and set aside.

2. Add the carrots, celery, rosemary and onion to the frying pan, season with salt and pepper and cook on a medium heat for 8 minutes until softened. Stir occasionally with a wooden spoon. Pour in the wine and continue to cook for a further 2 minutes to allow the alcohol to evaporate. With a wooden spoon, scrape all the good bits off the bottom of the frying pan. Pour in the chopped tomatoes with a glass of water and the olives and bring to the boil.

3. Transfer the sauce to an ovenproof dish and add the rabbit pieces. Cover with foil or a lid and cook in the oven for 1½ hours until the rabbit is tender and the sauce has thickened.

4. Before serving, season with salt and pepper and sprinkle over the parsley. Serve in a large warm serving dish with plenty of crusty bread around it. *Buon appetito!*

Marinated beef skewers with a three-bean salad / SPIEDINI DI MANZO MARINATO CON INSALATA AI TRE FAGIOLI

This is the perfect barbecue dish. I have used really flavoursome meat along with colourful veg so that each bite will give you a different taste and texture. The flavours of these simple ingredients are enhanced by fresh rosemary and zingy lemon and perfectly complemented by this delicious and healthy three-bean salad. This is absolutely not a dish to be saved for the summer; stick it on the griddle or under the grill and keep it on the menu all year round.

Serves 4

600g rump steak, cut into 2cm cubes
2 tablespoons honey
100ml red wine
5 fresh rosemary sprigs
2 red onions, peeled and cut into 8 chunks
2 yellow peppers, cut into 2cm cubes
2 courgettes, cut into 2cm rounds
1 tablespoon olive oil
1 x 400g tin cannellini beans, drained and rinsed
1 x 400g tin chickpeas, drained and rinsed
1 x 400g tin borlotti beans, drained and rinsed
4 tablespoons extra virgin olive oil
1 tablespoon white wine vinegar
Juice of 1 lemon
1 small red onion, finely sliced
3 tablespoons chopped fresh flat leaf parsley
Salt and freshly ground black pepper

1. First soak wooden skewers in water, if using, then place the meat in a bowl, pour over the honey and red wine. Remove the leaves of the rosemary from the stalks then add these. Stir well before seasoning well with black pepper only. Leave to marinate for 1 hour at room temperature.

2. After an hour, start to make up the skewers by threading the meat and vegetables onto the soaked wooden skewers – or use metal ones. You can put as much meat or vegetables on as you like. Once you have made the skewers brush with a little olive oil, then place on a hot griddle pan or BBQ. Once golden brown on one side turn over, trying not to turn them too often.

3. Whilst the meat is cooking make the salad. Place the beans in a large bowl, then add the extra virgin olive oil, white wine vinegar, lemon juice, red onion and parsley. Season with salt and black pepper. Stir everything together.

4. Once the meat is cooked remove from the BBQ or griddle and leave to rest for 5 minutes, allowing the meat to relax, then sprinkle with a little salt and serve alongside your three-bean salad.

Proper northern Italian meatballs / POLPETTE

Meatballs are a great meal to prepare and, if you are busy, are equally as nice prepared in the morning or the day before, allowing you to just come in from work and heat them through. I absolutely love the combination of lamb and pork; it gives the meatballs a new flavour dimension instead of always using just minced beef. It's just another option that gives you the same concept but with completely different results. You can replace the Pecorino with Parmesan if you prefer or add in a teaspoon of caramelised onion, which is *fantastico*.

Serves 4

300g minced pork
300g minced lamb
3 garlic cloves, peeled and crushed
150g fresh white breadcrumbs
5 tablespoons chopped fresh flat leaf parsley
80g freshly grated Pecorino cheese
Salt and black pepper to taste
2 eggs
Olive oil for greasing

For the sauce
2 x 720ml bottles of passata (sieved tomatoes)
3 tablespoons extra virgin olive oil
A few fresh basil leaves

1. Preheat the oven to 220°C/gas mark 7. Brush a large baking tray with oil and set aside.

2. In a large mixing bowl, combine the pork, lamb, garlic, breadcrumbs, parsley and Pecorino. Season with salt and pepper and break in the eggs. Mix all the ingredients together thoroughly with your hands, then shape into 12 equal-sized balls (around 75g each). Place the balls onto the oiled baking tray and bake in the oven for 15 minutes until cooked through.

3. Meanwhile, make the sauce. Pour the passata into a large saucepan with the extra virgin olive oil and place over a medium heat. Season with salt and pepper, add in the basil and bring to the boil. Lower the heat and gently simmer for 10 minutes with the lid half on. Stir occasionally with a wooden spoon.

4. Remove the meatballs from the baking tray and drop them into the tomato sauce. Continue to cook on a low heat for 30 minutes with the lid half on. Stir occasionally and if the sauce gets too thick, add a little hot water.

5. Serve hot or at room temperature with plenty of warm ciabatta bread to do the 'Scarpetta' (i.e. mop up the sauce).

Modena-style trio of meats with chilli and rosemary / TRIS DI CARNE ALLA MODENESE

My trip to Modena inspired me to use their top three cuts of meat all together in a tomato-based sauce. Here I have taken a northern Italian dish and added a southern Italian twist by using tinned tomatoes. This is delicious, and because of the long, slow cooking process the meat is left melting in your mouth. You can vary the amount of chilli according to your taste.

Serves 4

4 tablespoons olive oil
1 large onion, peeled and finely sliced
2 tablespoons fresh rosemary leaves
½ teaspoon dried chilli flakes
350g topside of beef, cut into 2cm chunks
8 large pork ribs, cut in half
4 Italian-style pork sausages
3 x 400g tins chopped tomatoes
2 tablespoons tomato purée
10 fresh basil leaves
Salt to taste
8 slices of ciabatta bread
2 garlic cloves, peeled

1. Heat the oil in a large heavy-based saucepan and cook the onion with the rosemary and chilli for 5 minutes. Stir occasionally with a wooden spoon. Add in the beef, ribs and sausages and continue to cook on a medium heat for 5 minutes until the meats are browned all over.

2. Pour in the chopped tomatoes, tomato purée and basil. Mix all together, bring to the boil then lower the heat to a simmer. Cover with a lid and cook very gently for 2 hours until the sauce is thick and shiny. Stir the sauce every 20 minutes, then remove the lid for the last 30 minutes of cooking. At the end of the cooking time, season the sauce with salt.

3. Toast the slices of ciabatta on both sides and rub the garlic all over.

4. Serve my trio of meats on a beautiful rustic platter accompanied with the toasted garlic bread and a nice bottle of Italian red wine.

T-bone steak with courgette ribbons and goat's cheese /

TAGLIATA ALLA FIORENTINA CON STRISCE DI ZUCCHINE E FORMAGGIO DI CAPRA

I believe that if you want to eat the very best steak in the world, you have to go to Florence. Tuscan meat is divine – and the locals know how to cook it to perfection.

Serves 2–3

700g T-bone steak
Olive oil
1 garlic bulb, cut in half

For the courgette ribbons
3 courgettes, cut into ribbons using a
  vegetable peeler
½ red chilli, deseeded and finely sliced
1 tablespoon white wine vinegar
2–3 tablespoons extra virgin olive oil
2 garlic cloves, finely sliced
20 small fresh mint leaves
60g soft and crumbly goat's cheese

1. Heat a griddle pan on a high heat. Make two cuts into the fat of the steak then rub the whole thing with a little oil. Transfer the meat to the griddle pan and cook for 2 minutes, then make a quarter turn (on the same side) and cook for a further 2 minutes – this will give you a criss-cross pattern on the steak. Rub each cut half of the garlic with a little oil, then place on the griddle pan. After 4 minutes of cooking, turn the steak over and repeat on the other side, turning the garlic as well.

2. Meanwhile, put the courgette ribbons in a large bowl and add the chilli, white wine vinegar, extra virgin olive oil and garlic, then tear the mint leaves into the bowl and toss together. Season with pepper and set aside, stirring occasionally.

3 Once the steak is cooked how you like it, remove it from the pan and leave to rest for at least 5 minutes. Then, using a sharp knife, remove the fillet steak and sirloin steak from the bone and slice the meat on an angle. Season with salt and a little black pepper.

4. Gently crumble the goat's cheese into the courgettes, season with salt and carefully mix through. Serve the steak on a rustic board with the garlic, the courgette ribbons and a final drizzle of extra virgin olive oil.

Lamb escalopes with wild mushrooms and white wine /

SCALOPPINE D'AGNELLO AI FUNGHI E VINO BIANCO

Whenever I prepare this recipe everyone says it's amazing and believes it has taken ages – when in reality it is so incredibly easy to prepare and takes less than twenty minutes from start to finish. It is a really tasty, creamy dish that everyone who has tried it absolutely loves. You can omit the wild mushrooms if you prefer, but I had to add them, not only because while travelling around northern Italy I realised how important an ingredient they are, but also because their flavour really takes the dish from being great to amazing.

Serves 4

500g lamb fillet, cut into 4 medallions
Olive oil
2 garlic cloves, peeled and slightly crushed
1 tablespoon fresh rosemary leaves
300g fresh wild mushrooms, washed and dried
Salt and black pepper to taste
50g plain flour
4 tablespoons white wine
200ml beef stock, made with stock cubes
15g salted butter

1. Place the lamb medallions between two layers of cling film and bash with a mallet until they are flattened and about 2mm thick. Set aside.

2. Heat 4 tablespoons of oil in a large frying pan over a high heat and fry the garlic and rosemary for 30 seconds. Add in the mushrooms and continue to fry for 3 minutes, stirring occasionally. Transfer the mushrooms to a warm plate and set aside. Wipe the frying pan with kitchen paper, ready to be used again.

3. Season the escalopes on both sides with salt and pepper. Coat each escalope in the flour and shake off any excess. Place the frying pan back over a medium heat and pour in 4 tablespoons of oil. Fry the lamb escalopes for 1 minute on each side. Pour in the wine and cook for a minute to allow the alcohol to evaporate. Add in the mushroom mixture, stir in the stock and continue to cook for a further 3 minutes. Stir in the butter for 30 seconds to thicken the sauce.

4. Place the escalopes in the middle of a warm serving plate, top with the wild mushrooms and pour over the juices from the pan. Serve immediately with lots of crusty bread to mop up the sauce.

PIZZA & BREAD

It's amazing that something as simple as a mixture of water and flour has fed populations for centuries and yet we never tire of the variations that it offers. Bread is an extremely serious staple in the Italian food chain and has been for years. You will never sit down at a table for lunch or dinner without a basket of bread before you.

The Romans were the first bakers to refine milling practices to produce white bread that was perfect for religious rituals – so much so that ovens were even built in some temples. This wonderful creation, which so many of us could just not live without, started with three simple ingredients: water, flour and yeast – but today we also include soy beans, mixed grains and corn, let alone the multitude of other ingredients that we add to create different tastes and textures.

Throughout this book we have already seen the vast variations in food from region to region, but when it comes to bread, the choice is absolutely massive. There are more than three hundred types of bread in Italy, and the most popular in the north are ciabatta, *pane nero di Coimo*, focaccia and *michetta*, to name but a few. One particular regional difference is the use of salt; some areas don't use it at all in bread, which is a throwback to the days when there was a tax on salt, so the bakers rebelled and refused to use it.

Most breads today are still baked in brick ovens, and pizzas are also best cooked this way. Pizzas originated in the south, but now they are popular everywhere in Italy and I would say it is the toppings that differ between regions rather than the dough and cooking techniques. The one thing I noticed that the whole of Italy had in common is that they never pre-slice your pizza and it is never eaten using a knife or fork, so when making my chosen recipes, tear your breads and use your hands to eat each slice. I promise you, somehow it makes eating it so much more enjoyable.

Piedmont pizza with Taleggio and parsley / PIZZA ALLA PIEMONTESE

I sampled this pizza whilst on my travels and the reason it has made it into this chapter is because I genuinely wasn't sure I was going to like it. I was pleasantly surprised. This is a tomato-based pizza, which is not so different, but, OK, Taleggio cheese rather than mozzarella? It has a slightly stronger flavour, which works. And then parsley? Not basil or oregano, but parsley? Weird? No! It is fantastic and you must try it.

Makes 2 pizzas

150g passata (sieved tomatoes)
150g tinned chopped tomatoes
Salt and black pepper to taste
Extra virgin olive oil
200g strong plain flour, plus extra for dusting
7g fast-action dried yeast
300g Taleggio cheese, rind removed and cut
  into little cubes
4 tablespoons whole fresh flat leaf parsley

1. Combine the passata, tomatoes and 2 tablespoons of oil in a bowl. Season and set aside.

2. Brush 2 baking trays each with 1 tablespoon of oil and brush the inside of a large bowl with another tablespoon of oil. Set aside.

3. Prepare the dough by placing the flour, yeast and a pinch of salt into a large clean bowl, make a well in the centre and pour in 140ml of water with 2 tablespoons of oil. Use a wooden spoon to mix everything together and create a wet dough. Turn out onto a clean well-floured surface and work it with your hands for about 5 minutes or until smooth and elastic. Shape into a large ball and place in the oiled bowl. Brush the top of the ball with a little oil and cover with cling film. Leave to rest for 20 minutes.

4. Preheat the oven to 220°C/gas mark 7. Once rested, turn out the dough onto a well-floured surface and divide it into two balls. Use your hands to push each out from the centre, creating two round discs about 25cm in diameter. Place the pizza bases on the two oiled baking trays. Spread the bases equally with the tomato mixture – the best way to do this is to pour the sauce into the middle of the pizza base and spread it outwards from the centre using the back of a tablespoon.

5. Scatter the Taleggio over the pizzas. Cook in the middle of the oven for 14 minutes, until golden and brown. One minute before the end of cooking, scatter over the parsley and continue to cook. Serve hot.

Pizza with courgettes, chilli and fresh mint / PIZZA CON ZUCCHINE, PEPERONCINO E MENTA

Mint and courgettes have been married together for years, so why not make them a pizza topping? This recipe is a bit of a surprise, though, because just as your guests get a cheesy yet fresh taste in their mouths – bang, in comes the chilli. It's something really different from the traditional options and for me, it's a combination made to last forever. I have also used goat's cheese, which is *fantastico*.

Makes 2 pizzas

Extra virgin olive oil
200g strong plain flour, plus extra for dusting
7g fast-action dried yeast
Salt to taste
2 mozzarella balls, drained and sliced (not buffalo mozzarella)
2 tablespoons freshly grated Pecorino cheese
1 large courgette, discard top and bottom
1 large fresh red chilli, deseeded and finely chopped
10 fresh mint leaves

1. Brush two baking trays each with 1 tablespoon of oil and brush the inside of a large bowl with another tablespoon of oil. Set aside.

2. Prepare the dough by placing the flour, yeast and a pinch of salt into a separate large clean bowl, make a well in the centre and pour in 140ml water with 2 tablespoons of oil. Use a wooden spoon to mix everything together and create a wet dough. Turn out onto a clean well-floured surface and work it with your hands for about 5 minutes or until smooth and elastic. Shape into a large ball and place in the oiled bowl. Brush the top of the dough ball with a little oil and cover with cling film. Leave to rest at room temperature for 20 minutes.

3. Preheat the oven to 220°C/gas mark 7. Once rested, turn out the dough onto a well-floured surface and divide it into two balls. Use your hands to push each out from the centre, creating two round discs about 25cm in diameter. Place the pizza bases on the two oiled baking trays.

4. Scatter the mozzarella and Pecorino equally on top of the two pizzas. Then, using a potato peeler, finely slice the courgette into ribbons and place on top of the cheese. Sprinkle over the chilli, season with a little salt and drizzle over with olive oil. Cook in the middle of the oven for 14 minutes until the cheese is bubbling. One minute before the end of the cooking, scatter over the mint leaves and continue to cook. Serve hot with a glass of chilled Italian white wine.

White pizza with potatoes, rosemary and mascarpone cheese / PIZZA BIANCA CON PATATE, ROSMARINO E MASCARPONE

Yep, you have read the title right: potatoes on a pizza... I know they say you must never trust a man who says 'trust me', but please, trust me on this – it is incredible! OK, we are definitely catering for the carb lover here, but it is so worth it. I have often sneaked in a few slices of salami too, which makes a winning combination. Even if you try this once and eat salad for the rest of the week, treat yourself and just do it – you won't regret it.

Makes 2 pizzas

Extra virgin olive oil
1 large waxy potato, peeled and very thinly
  sliced
200g strong plain flour, plus extra for dusting
7g fast-action dried yeast
Salt and black pepper to taste
300g mascarpone cheese, room temperature
3 tablespoons fresh rosemary leaves

1. Brush two baking trays each with 1 tablespoon of oil and brush the inside of a large bowl with another tablespoon of oil. Set aside.

2. Place the potato in a small saucepan with boiling water and cook for 30 seconds. Drain and rinse immediately under cold water. Set aside.

3. Prepare the dough by placing the flour, yeast and a pinch of salt into a large clean bowl, make a well in the centre and pour in 140ml water with 2 tablespoons of oil. Use a wooden spoon to mix everything together and create a wet dough. Turn out onto a clean well-floured surface and work it with your hands for about 5 minutes or until smooth and elastic. Shape into a large ball and place in the oiled bowl. Brush the top of the dough ball with a little oil and cover with cling film. Leave at room temperature to rest for 20 minutes.

4. Preheat the oven to 220°C/gas mark 7. Once rested, turn out the dough onto a well-floured surface and divide it into two balls. Use your hands to push each out from the centre, creating two round discs about 25cm in diameter. Place the pizza bases on the two oiled baking trays.

5. Spread the mascarpone equally over the pizzas and scatter over the potato slices. Sprinkle with the rosemary leaves, season with salt and drizzle with olive oil. Cook in the middle of the oven for 14 minutes. Serve hot or warm accompanied by your favourite salad.

186

Traditional folded bread with Genovese pesto / PIEGATA TRADIZIONALE ALLA GENOVESE

Freshly baked bread and pesto are a must-have in the north of Italy, and I can see why this combination is so popular. The fresh simple pesto taste just gives the bread a wonderful flavour. Please, please make sure you buy a really good-quality pesto or, even better, make your own. It really will make a huge difference to the end product and remember, once a jar of pesto is opened the flavours are never quite the same a few days later.

Makes 4 pieces

Extra virgin olive oil
500g strong plain flour, plus extra for dusting
5g fast-action dried yeast
2 teaspoons sea salt
1 teaspoon freshly ground black pepper
1 teaspoon caster sugar
4 tablespoons Genovese basil pesto
4 tablespoons freshly grated Pecorino cheese

1. Brush the inside of a large bowl with 1 tablespoon of oil and set aside.

2. Prepare the dough by placing the flour, yeast and a pinch of salt into another large clean bowl, make a well in the centre and pour in 300ml of warm water with 2 tablespoons of oil. Use a wooden spoon to mix everything together and create a wet dough.

3. Turn out onto a clean, well-floured surface and work the dough with your hands for about 5 minutes or until smooth and elastic. Shape into a large ball and place in the oiled bowl. Brush the top of the ball with a little oil and cover the bowl with cling film. Leave at room temperature to rest for 20 minutes.

4. Preheat the oven to 180°C/gas mark 4. Once rested, turn out the dough onto a well-floured surface and divide it into 4 equal pieces. Shape into round balls and leave to rest for 20 minutes on the work surface. With your fingertips, gently start to press the dough out, extending each piece to form a 1cm thick circle. Place the circles on a lightly floured baking tray.

5. Spread 1 tablespoon of pesto on each dough circle and sprinkle over 1 tablespoon of Pecorino. Take the edge of each dough circle and fold over loosely to form a half-moon shape – do not seal the edges. Leave to rise in the baking tray for 30 minutes. Bake the piegata in the middle of the oven for 17–20 minutes until the bread is golden brown. Serve warm with a cold glass of Italian beer.

Calzone with ricotta cheese and Parma ham / CALZONE RICOTTA E PROSCIUTTO CRUDO

Although a calzone is basically a pizza folded in half, it really feels more special than that. The inside is always a mystery and could contain anything from a creamy mushroom, sausage and spinach filling to a simpler cheese and ham option. I have chosen one of my favourites, but to be honest anything goes, and once you master the art of pizza dough, you can be as creative as you like. I have often added rocket leaves to this recipe and it tastes great.

Makes 2 folded pizzas

300g ricotta cheese, room temperature
Salt and black pepper to taste
Extra virgin olive oil
200g strong plain flour, plus extra for dusting
7g fast-action dried yeast
6 slices of Parma ham
8 cherry tomatoes, cut in half

1. Place the ricotta in a bowl and season with salt and pepper. Work it with the back of a fork until creamy and easy to spread. Set aside.

2. Brush two baking trays with 1 tablespoon of oil and brush the inside of a large bowl with another tablespoon of oil. Set aside.

3. Prepare the dough by placing the flour, yeast and a pinch of salt into a separate large clean bowl, make a well in the centre and pour in 140ml of warm water with 2 tablespoons of oil. Use a wooden spoon to mix everything together and create a wet dough. Turn out onto a clean well-floured surface and work it with your hands for about 5 minutes or until smooth and elastic.

Shape into a large ball and place in the oiled bowl. Brush the top of the dough ball with a little oil and cover with cling film. Leave at room temperature to rest for 20 minutes.

4. Preheat the oven to 220°C/gas mark 7. Once rested, turn out the dough onto a well-floured surface and divide it into two balls. Use your hands to push each out from the centre, creating two round discs about 25cm in diameter. Place the pizza bases on the two oiled baking trays.

5. Spread the ricotta equally over half of each pizza base using the back of a tablespoon. Arrange the slices of Parma ham on top, then fold the empty half of each base over to enclose the filling. Pinch the edges to seal and turn inwards, making tucks at regular intervals, to create a rope-like effect. Brush each calzone with oil and sprinkle over a little black pepper. Divide the halved cherry tomatoes on top. Cook in the middle of the oven for 14 minutes, until golden and brown. Serve hot and enjoy.

Pizza filled with Taleggio and rocket / PIZZA RIPIENA DI RUCOLA E TALEGGIO

This is not a calzone and can't be classified as a bread, but then again it isn't quite a pizza either. What I can tell you, though, is that it's worth preparing. I have used Taleggio cheese here rather than the traditional mozzarella because it is the favoured cheese in the north of Italy, being one of the oldest soft cheeses which is produced every autumn and winter. Although extremely pungent, it also has a salty, fruity taste and goes fantastically well with the other ingredients used in this recipe. If you want a stronger flavoured cheese, you could use its sister, Gorgonzola.

Serves 2

Extra virgin olive oil
200g strong plain flour, plus extra for dusting
7g fast-action dried yeast
Salt and black pepper to taste
150g ricotta cheese
¼ nutmeg
150g Taleggio cheese, rind removed
150g rocket leaves
3 tablespoons toasted pine nuts

1. Brush a large baking tray with 1 tablespoon of oil and brush the inside of a large bowl with another tablespoon of oil. Set aside.

2. Prepare the dough by placing the flour, yeast and a pinch of salt in a large clean bowl, make a well in the centre and pour in 140ml water with 1 tablespoon of oil. Use a wooden spoon to mix everything together to create a wet dough. Turn out onto a clean well-floured surface and work it with your hands for about 5 minutes or until smooth and elastic. Place in the oiled bowl, brush the top with a little more oil and cover with cling film. Leave at room temperature to rest for 20 minutes.

3. Preheat the oven to 200°C/gas mark 6. Once rested, turn out the dough onto a well-floured surface and divide it into two. Use your hands to push each out from the centre, creating two round discs about 20cm in diameter. Place one disc on the oiled baking tray.

4. Spread the ricotta over the pizza base using the back of a tablespoon, season with salt and pepper and grate over the nutmeg. Scatter over the Taleggio, rocket leaves and pine nuts.

5. Gently lift the second disc and place it on top of the filled one. Bring together the edges to enclose the filling. Pinch to seal and turn over the edges to create a rope-like effect. Brush the top of the filled pizza with oil. Cook in the middle of the oven for 18 minutes, until golden and brown. Serve hot with your favourite bottle of Italian red wine.

Ligurian loaf with Taggiasca black olives / FILONE CON OLIVE

TAGGIASCA

I cannot tell you the satisfaction you will feel when you make your own bread – and the smell of it cooking in your kitchen is to die for. Your guests will think you have become a master chef and yet, other than being a little time-consuming as you have to wait for the dough to rise, it really is quite simple to do. This crunchy olive bread is absolutely perfect with a bowl of soup or some antipasti. Eating it warm is definitely the perfect way to serve it.

Makes 1 loaf

Extra virgin olive oil
325g strong white flour
7g fast-action dried yeast
1 teaspoon salt
210ml warm water
150g Taggiasca pitted black olives,
  roughly chopped

1. Brush a baking tray and the inside of a large bowl with 1 tablespoon of oil.

2. Place the flour, yeast and a pinch of salt into another large clean bowl, make a well in the centre and pour in the water with 2 tablespoons of oil. Use a wooden spoon to mix everything together and create a wet dough. Turn out onto a clean well-floured surface and work it with your hands for about 10 minutes or until smooth and elastic. Shape it into a large ball and place in the oiled bowl. Cover with cling film and leave it to rise for 1 hour in a warm place away from draughts.

3. Turn the dough out onto a lightly floured surface and punch down. Flatten it out and sprinkle over the Taggiasca olives. Fold up and knead again for 2 minutes. Leave the dough to rest for 5 minutes then shape into an oval loaf and place on the oiled baking tray. With the help of a sharp knife, make 6 deep cuts on the top of the loaf. Brush the top with a little oil and cover with cling film. Leave it to rise for 40 minutes in a warm place away from draughts.

4. Preheat the oven to 200°C/gas mark 6. Brush the top of the loaf with more oil and bake in the middle of the oven for 35 minutes.

5. Transfer to a wire rack to cool and serve warm or at room temperature to accompany your favourite Italian antipasti. *Buon appetito*!

cont

insa

SIDES & SALADS

When I first came to England I was really surprised at how side dishes and salads were served. Everything always gets piled up onto one plate at each meal, which, in my opinion, just ends up giving you one flavour rather than the three or four you were supposed to have – especially if there is a creamy sauce or gravy involved. In Italy, whatever region you are in, your side and salad dishes are always served separately, to allow the individual flavours of each vegetable to stand out in their own right. Even roast potatoes would not be served on the same plate as your roast chicken or your veal Milanese, and I am a true believer that this is how accompaniments should be served.

Northern Italian side dishes vary not only from region to region but from season to season. Unlike most places in Europe, it is very hard to find a vegetable or fruit in the north if it is not their time to be harvested. Most side dishes usually comprise a variety of either grilled, sautéed, roasted or pickled vegetables – artichokes, aubergines, asparagus, mushrooms and spinach are top choices in most restaurants, with potato

options coming a close second. We have the same approach with salads, too. It's very rare (unless you are in a very touristy area) to find a salad with loads of ingredients in it. I actually really enjoy big, busy salads, but in Italy you are still likely to find individual ingredients, such as a simple tomato salad, or in Venice the amazing radicchio lightly grilled and seasoned with local herbs and olive oil.

There is a huge respect for accompaniments in Italy and no main meal is served without them.

There are so many incredible side dishes to choose from and it would have been impossible to narrow it down to my favourites as I love them all, so here I have selected just some of the dishes that myself and the crew experienced on our travels, and I hope this gives you a taste of northern Italy.

Spicy potato salad / INSALATA DI PATATE PICCANTE

I do love the way that potato salad is served in the UK, but sometimes all the mayonnaise distracts from the beautiful earthy flavour of the potato. This is such a lovely way to make this iconic salad – let the potato speak for itself! Amazing as a side dish or even better the day after to take to the office.

Serves 4

2 large potatoes
Salt
2 tablespoons olive oil
2 garlic cloves, peeled and crushed
2 red chilli peppers, deseeded and finely chopped
2 tablespoons extra virgin olive oil
3 tablespoons chopped fresh flat leaf parsley

1. Place the potatoes, unpeeled, in a medium saucepan and cover with water and 1 teaspoon of salt. Bring to the boil, cover and simmer for 40 minutes or until the potatoes are cooked. Insert a knife into the centre of each potato – if it is soft, it is cooked. Remove from the heat and slice into 1cm discs when cool enough to handle. Place in a bowl while you prepare the rest of the ingredients.

2. Heat the olive oil in a small saucepan and add the garlic and chilli. Fry for 3 minutes or until the garlic starts to colour. Take off the heat then pour in the olive oil. Pour over the potatoes and season with salt. Add in the parsley and gently mix everything together.

3. Transfer to a large serving dish and serve hot or at room temperature.

Tuscan-style roasted potatoes with red onions / PATATE ALLA TOSCANA

The potato originated in South America and in Italy it is mostly cultivated in the south – in Puglia, Campania and Calabria – but also in the Veneto region in the north, where the soil is perfect for a good crop. This is such a quick and simple dish yet it makes my kitchen smell as though I've been slaving away for hours. It goes perfectly with any fish or meat dish.

Serves 6

900g new potatoes, unpeeled
Salt and black pepper to taste
100ml olive oil
3 large garlic cloves, unpeeled and crushed
2 tablespoons fresh rosemary leaves
3 large red onions, peeled and cut into quarters

1. Preheat the oven to 180°C/gas mark 4. Wash the potatoes and place in a large saucepan, cover with cold water and add 1 tablespoon of salt. Bring to the boil and cook for 15 minutes. Drain, and cut each potato in half.

2. Pour the olive oil into a large ovenproof dish. Add the garlic and rosemary and swirl them around to mix the flavours. Add the hot potatoes with the onions and coat everything in the flavoured oil. Season with salt and pepper and roast for 45 minutes, turning halfway through.

Crushed potatoes with garlic, sage and rosemary / PATATE GRATINATE

CON AGLIO, SALVIA E ROSMARINO

These potatoes have all the flavours of Italy – fresh herbs and juicy garlic, slightly oozing with warm olive oil. They are fantastic with grilled meats, chicken or fish and are so easy to prepare – just one big dish of deliciousness.

Serves 4

1kg potatoes (Maris Piper will do the job),
  peeled and cut into 4cm chunks
2 tablespoons olive oil
25g salted butter
3 garlic cloves, unpeeled and squashed
10 fresh sage leaves
2 fresh rosemary sprigs
Salt and black pepper to taste

1. Preheat the oven to 180°C/gas mark 4. Put the potatoes in a saucepan with 1 teaspoon of salt, fill with water and bring to the boil. Boil for 10 minutes, drain and set aside.

2. Pour the olive oil and the butter into an ovenproof dish together with the garlic, sage and rosemary. Put in the oven until the butter has melted.

3. Tip the potatoes into the butter and oil and give a good stir to coat. With a fork, gently crush each potato and season with salt and pepper. Roast for 30 minutes, turn the potatoes, then roast for a further 30 minutes. The potatoes should be crispy and golden and ready to be served hot.

Sautéed potatoes with garlic and thyme / PATATE IN PADELLA CON AGLIO E TIMO

This was my favourite potato dish when I was a child and it still is now. It was a huge treat to be taken to a restaurant when I was younger and on those occasions this dish was the one that I would always order. Food has come on in leaps and bounds in recent years but this dish always takes me back to a time when food – and life – seemed to be much simpler.

Serves 4

500g new potatoes, washed but not peeled
3 fresh thyme sprigs
3 garlic cloves, peeled and lightly crushed
Salt and black pepper to taste
3 tablespoons olive oil
100g salted butter, cubed

1. Place the potatoes, thyme and garlic in a large saucepan with 1 tablespoon of salt. Cover with water, bring to the boil and cook for 15 minutes until softened. Drain the potatoes and discard the thyme and garlic then cut each potato into three discs about 1cm thick.

2. Heat the oil in a large non-stick frying pan over a medium heat. When the oil is hot, place the potato discs in the pan and season with salt and pepper. Fry for 3 minutes then turn over, season with more salt and pepper and cook for a further 3 minutes. Add the butter to the pan and continue to fry until all the butter has melted. Coat the potatoes with the hot butter using a spoon. Serve immediately.

The ultimate tomato, pepper, artichoke and bread salad /

PANZANELLA

Panzanella is a Tuscan salad of bread and tomatoes that is very popular in the summer. It primarily includes chunks of soaked stale bread and tomatoes dressed with extra virgin olive oil and vinegar. However, get creative and add anything you please – cucumbers, capers, cheese or olives all work well. Do not use fresh bread for this or it will go soggy.

Serves 6

200g stale country-style loaf of bread, cut into
   2cm cubes
150g chargrilled peppers in oil, drained and
   roughly chopped
100g artichoke hearts in oil, drained and
   roughly chopped
6 ripe tomatoes, roughly chopped
1 red onion, peeled and finely sliced
2 celery sticks, finely chopped
20 fresh basil leaves, roughly chopped
6 tablespoons extra virgin olive oil
2 tablespoons white wine vinegar
Salt and freshly ground pepper to taste

1. Place the bread in a large mixing bowl and sprinkle with 8 tablespoons of cold water until moistened but not soggy. Add in the peppers, artichokes, tomatoes, onion, celery, basil, olive oil and vinegar. Season with salt and pepper and gently mix until all the ingredients are combined.

2. Serve in a big salad bowl to accompany any of your barbecue dishes.

Red pepper, Taleggio and courgette salad / INSALATONA DI PEPERONI, TALEGGIO E ZUCCHINE

This is definitely one of my favourite summer recipes ever – the heat from the courgettes makes the Taleggio ooze slightly, increasing the beautiful flavour. Every time I eat this salad it makes me feel like I'm on holiday. Happy days!

Serves 4

10 tablespoons chilli oil
4 tablespoons freshly squeezed lemon juice
25g chopped fresh mint leaves
25g chopped fresh flat leaf parsley
8 courgettes, discard top and bottom, slice
  thinly lengthways
2 x 290g jar chargrilled peppers in oil, drained
  and cut in half
400g Taleggio cheese, broken into little pieces,
  rind removed
Salt and black pepper to taste
50g toasted pine kernels

1. In a small bowl, whisk 8 tablespoons of chilli oil with the lemon juice, mint and parsley. Set aside.

2. Preheat a griddle pan until hot. Brush the courgette slices with the remaining chilli oil and cook on the griddle pan in batches for 1 minute on each side, until charred. Place all the courgettes in a large bowl and scatter over the peppers and Taleggio. Pour over the dressing while the courgettes are still warm, season with salt and pepper and toss everything together.

3. Divide the salad between four serving plates, scatter over the pine kernels and serve with lots of warm crusty bread.

Roasted tomatoes with balsamic vinegar / POMODORI AL FORNO CON ACETO BALSAMICO

The Italians have really taken the tomato to their hearts – and we eat approximately 50kg of tomatoes per head, per year. People in the north prefer their tomatoes to be almost green, so this recipe is ideal for bringing out the sweetness of this beautiful fruit through baking. This is perfect served alongside any meat dish.

Serves 6

700g mixed varieties of large and small tomatoes
2 garlic cloves, peeled and crushed
½ teaspoon caster sugar
125ml olive oil
2 tablespoons balsamic vinegar
10 small fresh basil leaves
Salt and freshly ground black pepper

1. Preheat the oven to 180°C/gas mark 4. Wash and dry the tomatoes. Cut a cross in the top of each large tomato and halve the little ones. Place in a large baking tray and set aside.

2. In a small bowl combine the garlic, sugar, olive oil and balsamic vinegar. Drizzle the dressing over the tomatoes and bake in the oven for 25 minutes until the tomatoes have softened and their juices are beginning to ooze.

3. Scatter over the basil leaves, season with salt and pepper and serve.

Baby leeks with peas and crispy Parma ham / PORRI E PISELLI ALLA CONTADINA

We grow peas in almost every region in Italy. I've used frozen peas in this recipe but you can use peas fresh from the pod if you prefer. This was served to me at a friend's house a few years ago and I was very impressed. Simple but very tasty. You can replace the Parma ham with sliced pancetta if you prefer.

Serves 4

25g salted butter
8 baby leeks, topped, tailed and washed
200ml hot chicken stock, made from stock cubes
400g frozen peas, defrosted
100ml double cream
2 tablespoons chopped fresh tarragon
90g Parma ham slices

1. Melt the butter in a large pan. Add the leeks and cook for 3 minutes or until just starting to colour. Stir occasionally with a wooden spoon. Pour in the stock, cover with a lid and simmer for 10 minutes. Add in the peas, cream and tarragon. Bring to the boil and simmer, uncovered, for 5 minutes.

2. Preheat the grill to high. Lay the Parma ham slices on a baking tray and place under the grill for 5 minutes, turning halfway through, until crisp.

3. Tip the leeks and peas into a large serving dish, break up the Parma ham slices and scatter on top to serve.

Baked rice with peas, pancetta and asparagus / RISO AL FORNO CON PISELLI, PANCETTA E ASPARAGI

Rice with peas and pancetta is one of Venice's great loves. They make it in the springtime with tiny young tender peas. Their version is moist and more soup-like than this recipe and they serve it as a first course. I've adapted my recipe to include delicious tender asparagus spears, which makes a fantastic side dish.

Serves 6

80g salted butter
1 onion, peeled and finely chopped
100g pancetta, diced
1 litre hot chicken stock, made from stock cubes
150g frozen peas, defrosted
bunch of thin asparagus spears, cut into
  3cm pieces
Salt and black pepper to taste
400g long grain rice

1. Preheat the oven to 180°C/gas mark 4. Melt the butter in a medium saucepan over a medium heat. Add the onion and pancetta and cook gently for 5 minutes. Stir occasionally and don't let the onions burn.

2. Pour in the stock with the peas and asparagus and bring to the boil. Season with salt and pepper. Add the rice and give it a good stir. Simmer for 10 minutes or until all of the water has been absorbed.

3. Transfer into an ovenproof dish and bake in the middle of the oven for about 22 minutes.

4. Serve hot to accompany your favourite fish or meat dish.

Savoy cabbage with pancetta and white wine / VERZA CON PANCETTA E VINO BIANCO

Most people have awful memories of cabbage from their schooldays, so I've devised a recipe that I hope will erase the thought of the old school dinner. The humble cabbage is, in my opinion, very very underrated in the UK. In Italy cabbage is eaten all over the country, but the Savoy cabbage is particularly popular with the people of Piedmont, Lombardy and Veneto.

Serves 4

3 tablespoons olive oil
1 red onion, peeled and finely sliced
75g pancetta, diced
3 tablespoons Italian white wine
750g Savoy cabbage, finely shredded
1 tablespoon caster sugar
2 bay leaves
280ml vegetable stock, made with stock cubes
Salt and white pepper to taste

1. Heat the oil in a large saucepan. Cook the onion and pancetta over a medium heat for 5 minutes. Stir occasionally with a wooden spoon. Pour in the wine and continue to cook for 2 minutes to allow the alcohol to evaporate. Add all the remaining ingredients, mix well and bring to the boil.

2. Simmer with the lid on for 25 minutes. Remove the lid and continue to simmer for a further 5 minutes. Stir occasionally with a wooden spoon. Discard the bay leaves, season with salt and pepper and serve.

Bean and asparagus salad with balsamic glaze / INSALATONA DI FAGIOLI E ASPARAGI

Asparagus is a vegetable loved by Italians. It only has a short season and I remember growing it with my grandfather as a boy. The spears grow as shoots out of the earth and I had to cut them when they reached about 8 centimetres high. Asparagus grows very quickly and if I forgot to cut the spears they would become too woody to eat and then my grandmother would put them in a vase to decorate the table.

Serves 4

400g asparagus tips
1 x 400g tin borlotti beans, drained
5 spring onions, sliced
3 tablespoons extra virgin olive oil
1 tablespoon white wine vinegar
½ teaspoon caster sugar
¼ teaspoon Dijon mustard
5 medium tomatoes, thinly sliced
Salt and freshly ground black pepper
Handful of fresh basil, roughly chopped
Balsamic glaze to garnish

1. Bring a medium saucepan of salted water to the boil. Drop in the asparagus and cook for 3 minutes until cooked but with some bite. Drain and drop into cold water to refresh them – this keeps them crunchy and retains their beautiful colour.

2. Rinse the borlotti beans in a sieve under cold water, drain, then dry with kitchen paper as best as you can. Transfer them to a bowl with the spring onions and set aside.

3. In a small bowl pour in the olive oil, vinegar, sugar and Dijon mustard. Whisk to form a salad dressing. Pour the dressing into the beans and spring onions and give it a good stir.

4. Tip out the beans onto a flat plate and arrange the sliced tomatoes on top. Drain and dry the asparagus and arrange on top of the tomatoes. Season with salt and black pepper and throw over the basil. Finish with a good drizzle of balsamic glaze.

Do.

ici*

DESSERTS

Just like all the other chapters in this book, and as with every other part of north Italian cuisine, desserts here are definitely more creamy and heavier than in the south. In the northern regions desserts tend to be really rich rather than really sweet, though. This is, of course, the home of creamy, sweet mascarpone which is layered with sponge in a bitter, alcoholic classic dessert, Tiramisu. It is a combination like no other, which is perhaps why Tuscany and Venice have fought over the origin of this recipe for years. However, most sources confirm that this dessert is a Venetian creation and it is definitely a firm favourite on their menus.

Fruits are also heavily used in northern desserts, but rather than served simply and raw, as in the south of Italy, they are often stewed or baked. A must-try on your travels through northern Italy are the dumplings or strudels that are on offer. Due to the Austrian and German influences on the cuisine here, some of the tastiest examples of these desserts are available in the fabulous bakeries or on market stalls.

It's funny, in the past, and especially when I was growing up, cakes and desserts were seen as a really special treat and were only served up on special occasions or festivals, but thank goodness over the years the sweet tooth of our population has made sure that desserts have become more of an everyday offering.

DESSERTS

We Italians also pride ourselves on our amazing ice creams, sorbets and granitas. No Italian cookbook would be complete without a couple of recipes, and no Italian restaurant is ever without a selection for you to choose from. These frozen desserts are such a huge part of our culinary culture, and, whether it's sitting on a beach or taking a *passeggiata* – our traditional evening walk around the cities and towns – even in the colder months an Italian ice cream is a definite must.

There were so many desserts to choose from when I toured the north... how could I narrow it down to just ten? Well, I didn't, I made it twelve – just for you. I decided to take a few of the most popular, a few of my favourites and hopefully some that might be a bit new to you. Enjoy!

Baked figs with honey and vanilla mascarpone / FICHI AL FORNO
CON MIELE E MASCARPONE ALLA VANIGLIA

Figs are a real Mediterranean favourite and are eaten all over Italy. Originally from Syria, the fig spread throughout the world via the Romans. Liguria grows the Gentile Bianco, which is probably the best-known variety in Italy. The walnuts here add a delicious crunch, but you could replace them with pistachios if you prefer. This recipe calls for vanilla-flavoured mascarpone as an accompaniment, but you could also serve the figs with a ball of soft vanilla ice cream.

Serves 4

12 ripe figs
50g salted butter
50g walnut halves
4 tablespoons runny honey
200g mascarpone cheese
1 teaspoon vanilla extract

1. Preheat the oven to 180°C/gas mark 4. Wash and dry the figs and cut a cross on the top of each so they fan out when gently squeezed. Transfer to an ovenproof dish and place a cube of butter inside each fig. Scatter the walnuts over the figs and drizzle with honey. Bake in the oven for 20 minutes until the figs are soft and oozing their juices, basting halfway through cooking.

2. Mix the mascarpone and vanilla together and transfer to a serving bowl.

3. Serve the figs hot accompanied with the vanilla mascarpone.

Cantaloupe melon granita /

GRANITA DI MELONE

With its juicy, sweet, orange-coloured pulp and green-grey skin, the cantaloupe melon is perfect for a granita. This melon variety is grown in the south and also in the northern region of Emilia-Romagna. For this recipe, choose the ripest melon you can. It is not always easy to tell if a melon is ripe, but try pressing both ends – it should be slightly soft and give off a fantastic aroma.

Serves 6

1 large cantaloupe melon
200g granulated sugar
3 clementines, rind and juices

1. Cut the melon in half and remove the seeds with a spoon. Remove and discard the skin and cut the flesh into chunks. Put the melon in a food processor and blitz until smooth.

2. Cut each clementine in half and squeeze the juice into a large bowl, retaining the rind.

3. Pour the sugar into a small heavy bottomed saucepan along with 4 tablespoons of water and the clementine rind. Slowly bring to the boil to dissolve the sugar then boil rapidly until the

mixture forms a sticky syrup and you can lift a short thread when the syrup is pulled between the back of two teaspoons. Remove the clementine rind and discard. Set aside to cool.

4. Add the melon purée, 300ml water and warm syrup to the large bowl of clementine juice. Mix and allow to cool.

5. Transfer to a shallow freezerproof container and freeze until ice starts to form around the edges. Whisk the granita mix with a fork until smooth and return to the freezer. Repeat the process every 20 minutes over the next 2 hours until there is no liquid left in the container and the mixture is just broken-up ice crystals.

6. Allow the granita to soften slightly before serving, so that it is easier to scoop out.

Ricotta mousse with chocolate and cinnamon sauce / MOUSSE DI RICOTTA CON CREMA AL CIOCCOLATO E CANNELLA

Ricotta cheese can be used in a huge variety of savoury and sweet dishes, it is so versatile and delicious. I've upped the measurements in the chocolate sauce in this recipe as it's so great poured over ice cream. Any leftovers are always gratefully received.

Serves 4

250g ricotta cheese
50g icing sugar
1 teaspoon vanilla extract
1 egg white
150ml double cream

For the chocolate sauce
50g cocoa powder
75g caster sugar
Pinch of salt
Pinch of ground cinnamon
100ml double cream

1. Place the ricotta, icing sugar and vanilla extract in a bowl and beat with an electric whisk until smooth. Set aside. In another clean bowl whisk the egg white until stiff. Set aside. In a third bowl whisk the cream until it forms soft peaks.

2. With the help of a spatula, fold the cream into the ricotta mixture. Gently fold in the egg white and be careful not to knock out the air. Spoon into dessert glasses or ramekins and chill for 2 hours.

3. Meanwhile, for the chocolate sauce, sift the cocoa powder into a small non-stick saucepan. Add the sugar, 100ml of water, salt and cinnamon. Bring to the boil, stirring continuously with a wooden spoon. Turn down the heat and continue to cook for 3 minutes, stirring continuously. Take the saucepan off the heat and stir in the cream. Leave to cool.

4. Drizzle the chocolate sauce over the ricotta mousse and serve immediately.

Coffee pots with melting chocolate / COPPE AL CAFFE' CON CIOCCOLATO FUSO

Italy's first coffee shop opened in Venice in 1640. Almost four hundred years later, we now consume huge quantities of this wondrous little bean. This recipe takes on the other favourite of all children (old and young)... chocolate. Together, coffee and chocolate are a match made in heaven.

Serves 6

200g self-raising flour
4 tablespoons cocoa powder, sieved
100g dark chocolate, chopped
200g caster sugar
2 pinches of ground cinnamon
50g melted salted butter
1 egg
175ml full-fat milk
6 tablespoons very strong coffee,
  preferably espresso

For the sauce
150g soft dark brown sugar
3 tablespoons cocoa powder, sifted
1 tablespoon instant coffee powder
260ml boiling water

1. Preheat the oven to 180°C/gas mark 4. In a large bowl, put the flour, cocoa powder, dark chocolate, caster sugar and cinnamon.

2. In a separate bowl, whisk the melted butter, egg, milk and coffee. Add the wet ingredients to the dry ingredients and stir to combine. Divide the mixture between 6 large ramekins, each about 300ml.

3. For the sauce, mix together the sugar, cocoa powder and instant coffee powder. Sprinkle this on top of the mixture in each of the ramekins to create a dry layer. Pour 3 tablespoons of boiling water from the kettle over each pudding on top of the coffee mixture and bake in the oven for 25 minutes. The result will be a spongy, chocolatey, saucy and gooey pudding.

4. Serve immediately with a little glass of Amaretto liqueur.

Chocolate ice cream with raisins and chocolate chips / GELATO AL

CIOCCOLATO CON UVETTA E GOCCE DI CIOCCOLATO

This recipe gets my heart racing – all my favourite things in one mouthful! This is a kid's ice cream for adults. Italians are constantly bringing out new flavours for ice cream, and no one does it quite like us!

Serves 4

50g raisins
3 tablespoons Cognac
4 large egg yolks
100g caster sugar
350ml full-fat milk
250ml double cream
200g dark chocolate
50g dark chocolate chips

1. Place the raisins in a small bowl and pour over the Cognac. Leave the raisins to soak while you prepare the rest of the ingredients.

2. In a large bowl beat together the egg yolks and sugar for about 5 minutes until thick, pale and creamy. Set aside.

3. In a medium saucepan, gently heat the milk and cream, stirring occasionally to prevent a skin forming. Take off the heat just before it starts to boil. Pour the milk mixture into the eggs very slowly, beating continuously. Return to the saucepan over a gentle heat and cook, stirring, for 15 minutes. Remove from the heat, pour into a bowl and leave to cool.

4. Break the dark chocolate into a small bowl and melt in the microwave in short bursts, stirring in between, or melt it in a heatproof bowl set over a pan of simmering water – do not let the base of the bowl touch the water. Add the melted chocolate to the milk and cream mixture and mix to combine.

5. Pour the chocolate mixture into a freezerproof shallow dish and place in the freezer for 2 hours. Remove from the freezer and add in the chocolate chips with the raisins and soaking Cognac. Gently mix through with a fork. Return to the freezer and take out after 20 minutes to fork through again. Repeat the same process three times. Enjoy!

227

Sweet pasta filled with ricotta, hazelnuts, orange and chocolate

/ MEZZALUNE DOLCI RIPIENE DI RICOTTA CON CIOCCOLATO, ARANCIA E NOCCIOLE

We love our pasta in Italy – so much so that we like to eat it for dessert too! These little half-moon-shaped pasta treats are perfect eaten at the end of a meal or with coffee or a chilled glass of sweet white wine. The combination of nuts, honey and chocolate make them very rich and perfect for festive entertaining.

Serves 4

For the pasta
2 large whole eggs, 1 egg yolk
250g '00' flour, plus a little for dusting
2 heaped tablespoons caster sugar
50g butter, softened
Olive oil, for frying

For the filling
250g ricotta cheese
Zest of 1 orange
50g finely chopped hazelnuts
50g good-quality dark chocolate chips
1 tablespoon caster sugar (optional)
1 egg, beaten
4 tablespoons honey, for drizzling
4 tablespoons icing sugar, for dusting

1. Beat together the eggs and egg yolk. Place the flour in a large bowl and add the sugar and butter, then add the eggs. With the end of a wooden spoon, bring the mix together, adding a drop of water if you need to. Once the mixture starts to come together, turn it out onto a clean work surface and start to knead the dough until the surface is clean and the dough smooth. Wrap in cling film and leave to rest for 20–30 minutes.

2. Meanwhile, combine the ricotta, orange zest, hazelnuts and chocolate chips, adding a tablespoon of sugar, if you like. Set aside.

3. Unwrap the chilled pasta dough onto a well-floured surface. Flatten it down slightly with your fingertips then roll it out until it is 2mm thick, or use a pasta machine – if you have one. Once thin, cut out 12 discs of pasta using a 10–12cm cutter. Brush around the edge of each disc with a little egg wash, then place a spoonful of the ricotta filling in the middle of each disc and fold the one half of the pasta circle over the filling, creating a half-moon shape. Press down firmly around the edge, then use a fork to press the edges together.

4. Heat 5cm oil in a saucepan. To check if the oil is hot, add a little offcut of pasta to the oil – if bubbles start to appear around it and it floats to the top, it is ready. Fry the half-moons in batches. Cook for 1½ minutes then carefully turn them over and cook for 1½ minutes on the other side. Remove with a slotted spoon and drain on kitchen paper. Serve immediately drizzled with honey and dusted with icing sugar.

Polenta cake with oranges and Cointreau / TORTA DI POLENTA CON ARANCE E COINTREAU

This is such a beautiful cake to enjoy in the afternoon with a cup of coffee or tea. Alternatively, serve it with a dollop of mascarpone on the side as a dessert. My kids, however, won't thank me for this recipe as they think every dessert should be about chocolate! You can substitute the Cointreau with a citrussy Limoncello if you prefer.

Serves 8

2 oranges
3 tablespoons Cointreau
5 eggs
250g caster sugar
100g polenta
175g ground almonds
1 teaspoon baking powder

For the orange syrup
100g caster sugar
Juice of 4 oranges
75ml Cointreau
1 cinnamon stick

1. Start by washing the two oranges, then place them in a small saucepan and cover with water. Bring to the boil and simmer for 1 hour. Remove from the water and set aside to cool slightly.

2. Preheat the oven to 180°C/gas mark 4. Line the base of a 23cm loose-bottomed cake tin with baking parchment. Cut the oranges in half and remove the pips. Place in a food processor or blender with the Cointreau and blitz for 10 seconds.

3. Place the eggs and sugar in a large bowl and whisk until the sugar has dissolved and the eggs are pale in colour. Fold in the oranges, polenta, ground almonds and baking powder. Pour the mixture into the tin and bake for 35–40 minutes. Cool in the tin and set aside.

4. To prepare the syrup, pour the sugar and 2 tablespoons of water into a small saucepan. Heat slowly until the sugar melts and caramel-coloured bubbles appear. Pour in the orange juice with the Cointreau and bring to the boil. Add the cinnamon stick and cook for 15 minutes more or until the liquid has reduced by half.

5. Remove the cooled cake from the tin and place on a serving plate. Using a wooden or metal skewer, make holes all over the top of the cake and pour half of the syrup into the holes. Serve the remaining syrup on the side.

Amaretti and chocolate mousse cake / TORTA FREDDA DI CIOCCOLATO E AMARETTI

I first had this cake at my best friend's house when I was about ten. His parents had invited friends over the night before and we were allowed to eat the leftovers – we finished it! I've tried to re-create it as best I could. Please try this mousse cake when you have friends over, but hide it from the children...

Serves 12

125g Amaretti biscuits, crushed
100g digestive biscuits, crushed
75g salted butter, melted
175ml full-fat milk
1 vanilla pod
400g dark chocolate
30ml very strong coffee (espresso, if you have it)
750ml double cream
Cocoa powder, sifted

1. Line the base of a 23cm loose-bottomed tin with baking parchment. Put half of the Amaretti biscuits and all of the digestive biscuits into a large bowl and pour over the melted butter. Stir, tip into the tin and press down with the back of a spoon. Transfer to the fridge for 2 hours to set.

2. Pour the milk into a small non-stick saucepan. Split the vanilla pod and scrape out the seeds with the back of a knife. Add these and the empty pods to the milk and bring to the boil. Simmer for a few minutes until the liquid has reduced to about 100ml. Set aside to cool slightly.

3. Meanwhile, place the chocolate in a bowl and melt in the microwave on High in short bursts, stirring in between, or melt it in a heatproof bowl set over a pan of simmering water – do not let the base of the bowl touch the water. When the chocolate is warm but not completely melted, stir to melt the last few solid squares of chocolate. Pour the coffee into the chocolate and mix.

4. Remove the vanilla pod from the milk and discard. Slowly pour the milk into the melted chocolate, stirring continuously. Set aside.

5. In a large clean bowl, whip the cream into soft peaks and fold into the chocolate mixture. Add the remaining Amaretti biscuits and stir.

6. Take the biscuit base out of the fridge and pour over the chocolate mousse. Smooth the top and return to the fridge for 5 hours. Just before serving, dust with cocoa powder.

Honey ice cream / GELATO AL MIELE VENEZIANO

Created from the nectar of bees, honey is the oldest natural sweetener known to man. Most honey is made from a range of hives but some types come purely from bees that have collected nectar from only one type of flower. The most popular single-flower honey is acacia and this is common in the region of Veneto. For this creamy, sweet ice cream you can use any runny honey, though. This is a really easy ice cream recipe, with no churning needed, and is amazing served with biscotti or simply on its own.

Serves 4

1 large egg
4 large egg yolks
100g runny honey
300ml double cream

1. Place the egg, egg yolks and honey in a heatproof bowl and set it over a saucepan of simmering water. Using a hand-held whisk, beat the mixture for 10 minutes until it becomes thick and pale.

2. In another bowl, beat the cream until it becomes stiff then, using a spatula, gently fold the cream into the honey mixture. Pour into a freezerproof container and freeze for 3 hours.

3. Take the ice cream out of the freezer 5 minutes before serving to allow it to soften.

Bitter chocolate and almond squares / QUADRATINI DI CIOCCOLATO E MANDORLE

I think this might be my showstopper cake – individual squares of perfection! Whenever I make this recipe my son Rocco covers me with kisses and on that day I am definitely the coolest dad EVER!!!

Serves 16

250g dark chocolate
250g salted butter, softened
250g caster sugar
6 eggs
250g ground almonds
300ml double cream, whipped

For the chocolate curls
150ml double cream
150g dark chocolate, broken up

1. To make the chocolate curls, pour the cream into a small non-stick saucepan and bring to the boil over a low heat. Add in the chocolate and continue to stir until it has all melted. Pour the mixture into a small flat dish and put in the fridge for 3 hours. Once set, fill a cup with hot water and dip in a teaspoon. Drag the spoon along the chocolate to form curls. Keep the curls in the fridge until they are ready to be used.

2. Preheat the oven to 160°C/gas mark 3. Line a 24cm square cake tin with baking parchment. Melt the chocolate in the microwave on High in short bursts, stirring in between, or melt it in a heatproof bowl set over a pan of simmering water – do not let the base of the bowl touch the water.

3. Cream the butter and sugar in a large mixing bowl with a hand-held mixer until light and fluffy. Add in the melted chocolate and mix thoroughly. Mix in the eggs, one at a time, then fold in the almonds. Pour into the prepared tin and bake for 40 minutes. When cooked, a piece of dry spaghetti inserted into the middle of the cake should come out clean. Leave the cake to cool in the tin then put it in the fridge for 1 hour to firm up.

4. Remove the cake from the tin, peel off the paper and cut into 16 squares. Place the chocolate squares on a large serving dish. Put a dollop of whipped cream on every square and top with a chocolate curl. Perfect served with a handful of fresh summer berries.

Chocolate Panforte with Amaretto liqueur / PANFORTE AL CIOCCOLATO

Siena is the panforte capital of Italy. This traditional dessert has been made since the thirteenth century in this ancient city, and is a spicy, sweet, fruity, nutty slab of deliciousness. The only thing that could beat it was the view from our hotel terrace of Siena's other wonder – the Duomo.

Serves 6

250g good-quality dark chocolate (70% cocoa solids)
3 egg whites
3 tablespoons runny honey
200g ground almonds
50g hazelnuts, skinless and roasted
100g walnuts
50g candied peel
4 tablespoons Amaretto liqueur

For the topping
100g good-quality dark chocolate (70% cocoa solids)
200g icing sugar
2 tablespoons icing sugar or sugar crystals to decorate

1. Line an 18cm round flan dish or cake tin with cling film. Melt the 250g of dark chocolate in a large heatproof bowl set over a pan of simmering water, making sure that the base of the bowl does not touch the water.

2. Lightly whisk the egg whites in a large clean bowl for 2 minutes – you just want to break them up rather than whisk them to a peak. Add the honey and whisk once more to incorporate.

3. Fold in the ground almonds with a large metal spoon and mix to a paste, then fold in the hazelnuts and walnuts. Stir in the mixed peel, Amaretto and icing sugar before very gently folding in the melted chocolate.

4. Pour the mixture into the tin, fold the cling film over the mixture and press everything down until smooth. Set aside in the fridge for 2 hours.

5. To make the topping, melt the chocolate in a heatproof bowl set over a pan of simmering water, making sure that the base of the bowl does not touch the water. Add 2 tablespoons of boiling water to the icing sugar, then add to the chocolate. Stir gently – you need to work quickly.

6. Turn out the cake onto a plate and peel off the cling film. Use a spatula to cover the surface with the chocolate syrup. Set aside for 1 hour until the chocolate has hardened, then dust with icing sugar or sprinkle with sugar crystals. Serve in slices with a cup of your favourite tea.

Classic Italian apple strüdel /

STRUDEL ITALIANO CLASSICO

This dessert is usually associated with Germany and Austria, but it is also often prepared in the northern regions of Italy. Although the classic strüdel is made with apples, it can also be made with other fruit fillings such as cherries, peaches or pears, depending on the time of year and what fruit is in season. A fantastic dessert that can be eaten warm or cold, as a pudding or served at teatime. You could make the filo pastry from scratch, but it is fiddly and time-consuming, so it's much easier to buy frozen or fresh filo pastry, which you can find anywhere.

Serves 6
4 tablespoons soft raisins
Zest and juice of 1 orange
800g cooking apples
50g salted butter
90g caster sugar
1 teaspoon ground cinnamon
1 teaspoon vanilla extract
Handful of fresh breadcrumbs

For the pastry
60g salted butter, melted
4 sheets filo pastry (about 30 x 37cm)
Icing sugar for dusting

1. Preheat the oven to 190°C/gas mark 5. Place the raisins in a small bowl with the orange zest and juice, and set aside to soak.

2. Peel the apples and discard the core. Cut into 1.5cm cubes and transfer to a small saucepan. Add the butter, 100ml of water and sugar and gently cook for 6 minutes, until the apples have softened but still retain their shape.

3. Remove from the heat and mix in the cinnamon and vanilla extract. Stir in the raisins with the juice and the breadcrumbs to combine. Set aside and leave to cool.

4. To make the pastry, brush a little melted butter over a large baking tray and place the first sheet of filo pastry in the greased tray. Keep the other filo sheets under a damp tea towel to prevent them drying out. Then brush the first sheet with a little more butter and repeat the process with the remaining sheets of pastry, placing them on top of each other.

5. Spoon the apple mixture along the middle of the pastry and carefully roll up the long sides around the filling, like a cigar. Tuck in the short ends and transfer to the baking tray, seam-side down. Brush all over with the remaining melted butter and bake in the oven for 20 minutes, until golden and crispy.

6. Dust with icing sugar and serve hot or warm with a dollop of mascarpone.

Apples poached in red wine with Amaretti biscuit cream /

MELE AL VINO ROSSO CON CREMA DI AMARETTI

Amaretti di Saronno is the most famous variety of these crunchy, almond-flavoured macaroons, and are traditional to the town of that name in the northern Italian commune of Lombardy and date back to the eighteenth century. In this recipe their crunchy crumbs make a fantastic contrast to soft, creamy mascarpone and lightly spiced poached apples. *Delizioso*.

Serves 4

4 large Granny Smith apples, peeled and
  cored but left whole
1¼ bottles Chianti
50g demerara or brown sugar
1 tablespoon black peppercorns
2 cinnamon sticks

For the biscuit cream
2 egg yolks
2 heaped tablespoons caster sugar
250g mascarpone cheese
1 vanilla pod, seeds scraped out
40g Amaretti biscuits (the crunchy ones),
  roughly crumbled

1. Place the apples in a medium saucepan – they should fit quite snugly – then pour in the wine (don't worry if the apples start to float). Add the sugar, peppercorns and cinnamon sticks and bring the wine to the boil. Gently boil for 4 minutes or until the apples are just tender. Remove the pan from the heat and leave the apples to cool in the wine – they will continue to cook, so turn them occasionally so that they take on an even colour, or place a small plate on top of them to keep them totally immersed in the wine.

2. Remove 2 ladles (about 150ml), of the spiced wine and transfer to a small saucepan. Simmer the liquid until reduced by half and syrupy, then leave to cool. The syrup will thicken as it cools.

3. When the apples are cold, make the Amaretti biscuit cream. Whisk the egg yolks and sugar together in a large bowl until pale and fluffy. Gently fold in the mascarpone and the seeds from the vanilla pod using a large metal spoon. Then fold in three-quarters of the Amaretti biscuits, reserving the rest for later.

4. Remove the cooled apples from the red wine and slice each one horizontally into 7 rings. Divide the apple rings among four plates, laying the rings of each apple in a circle, overlapping.

5. Put a couple of spoonfuls of the Amaretti cream in the middle of the apple rings, drizzle some red wine syrup around the apples, then scatter over the reserved Amaretti biscuits. Serve with a cup of your favourite tea.

Florentine biscuits / BISCOTTI

FIORENTINI

The Florentine was created in Florence during the Renaissance and was later exported to France. Today it is considered a typical French pastry, although many Italians would disagree. To us, it is an Italian biscuit made by setting nuts and dried fruit into a caramel disc, which is then often coated on the bottom with chocolate. Florentines are pretty much foolproof and, in my humble opinion, are the nicest biscuits in the world. You decide!

Makes 20

75g salted butter
100g golden caster sugar
50g plain flour
25g roasted hazelnuts, chopped
25g flaked almonds, toasted
30g glacé cherries, chopped
30g crystallised ginger, chopped
25g sultanas
25g mixed peel, chopped
150g dark chocolate

1. Preheat the oven to 180°C/gas mark 4. Line two large baking trays with baking parchment. Gently heat the butter and sugar together in a pan until the sugar dissolves. Mix in the flour then add the hazelnuts, almonds, cherries, ginger, sultanas and mixed peel.

2. Scoop teaspoons of the mixture onto the baking tray, leaving a 5cm space between each one – they will spread while baking. Flatten slightly with the back of the teaspoon and bake in the oven for 8 minutes.

3. While they are still hot, neaten the edges into a round shape with a knife. Leave to cool, then turn them over. Melt the chocolate in a microwave on High in short bursts, stirring in between, or melt it in a heatproof bowl set over a pan of simmering water – do not let the base of the bowl touch the water. Spread the melted chocolate on the flat side of the Florentines and leave to cool.

4. Serve with your favourite cup of tea or with a fantastic short espresso.

Lady's kisses / BACI DI DAMA

This is an Italian specialty from Turin. The name *Baci di Dama* literally means 'Lady's kisses', as the biscuits are paired together to resemble kissing lips. Make sure you don't spread the Nutella on the biscuits until they have completely cooled, otherwise it will just slide off.

Makes 10

120g salted butter, softened
120g caster sugar
1 teaspoon vanilla extract
120g ground almonds
120g '00' flour
10 teaspoons Nutella chocolate spread

1. Preheat the oven to 180°C/gas mark 4. In a large mixing bowl, beat the butter and sugar together until soft and creamy. Add the vanilla extract and beat again. Add the almonds and flour and work into the butter mixture until it forms a dough.

2. Divide the dough into four and then divide each piece into five. With floured hands roll each piece into a small ball and place on a baking tray lined with baking parchment, leaving a 3cm gap between each one. Flatten each ball slightly with the palm of your hand. Bake for 15 minutes until golden. Leave to cool on a wire rack.

3. When the biscuits are completely cool, sandwich two together with a teaspoon of Nutella. *Fantastico* served with a cappuccino.

Double chocolate, pistachio and chilli biscotti / BISCOTTI AL CIOCCOLATO, PISTACCHIO E PEPERONCINO

This is a perfect biscuit to dip into a caffè latte on the morning after the night before! Biscotti were originally made as a means of preserving bread by drying it. Baking them twice achieves this dryness. Today, biscotti are more of a biscuit – and so much more appealing.

Makes 40

200g plain flour, plus extra for dusting
60g cocoa powder
150g caster sugar
60g dark chocolate, chopped
½ teaspoon chilli powder
¾ teaspoon baking powder
½ teaspoon salt
3 eggs, lightly beaten
1 teaspoon vanilla extract
100g pistachio nuts
100g milk chocolate

1. Preheat the oven to 160°C/gas mark 3. Put the flour, cocoa powder, sugar, dark chocolate, chilli powder, baking powder and salt into a food processor and blitz for about 20 seconds. Add in the eggs and vanilla and pulse to form a dough.

2. Tip the dough onto a working surface dusted with flour. Knead the pistachios into the dough. Divide the dough into 4 and roll each piece into a 30cm sausage, then slightly flatten each piece with the palm of your hand. Place the four flattened sausage shapes onto a baking tray lined with baking parchment. Bake for 25 minutes. Cool for 5 minutes.

3. Using a sharp knife, diagonally cut each sausage into 10 pieces. Transfer the pieces back to the baking tray and leave a 2cm space between each piece. Bake for a further 15 minutes. Leave on the baking tray to cool.

4. Melt the milk chocolate in a microwave in short bursts, stirring in between, or melt it in a heatproof bowl set over a pan of simmering water – do not let the base of the bowl touch the water. Drizzle the melted chocolate over the biscotti using a fork. Leave to set on the baking tray then transfer to a large plate to serve.

Pear and banana sweet bread /

DOLCE CON PERE E BANANE

My wife often used to go out and buy small brioches or sweet breads as a snack for the kids, until I created this recipe; now my pear and banana bread is baked at least once every ten days in the D'Acampo household. The process is so quick and easy but the effect is very wow. It is absolutely delicious and never lasts more than twenty-four hours in our house. We've eaten it for breakfast, snacks or even when having people over for tea, and no one can believe how easy it is to make when they are given the recipe. You can replace the pears with mangoes if you prefer, but if you are being creative with fruit, make sure you do not use one that is too juicy, like an orange.

Serves 6

140g salted butter at room temperature,
   plus extra for greasing
150g soft brown sugar
2 eggs, beaten
2 ripe large bananas, mashed
2 ripe pears, peeled, core removed, cut into
   1cm cubes
100g pistachio nuts, roughly chopped
250g strong white flour
1 tablespoon baking powder
Pinch of salt
2 teaspoons vanilla extract

1. Preheat the oven to 180°C/gas mark 4. Grease a 1kg loaf tin with butter and line the base with baking parchment.

2. Cream the butter and sugar in a large bowl and whisk together until fluffy and pale in colour. In three stages, pour in the eggs, whisking well after each addition. Add the bananas, pears and pistachios to the mixture. Sift the flour and baking powder onto the mixture and add in the salt. Add the vanilla extract and gently fold everything together until all the ingredients are just combined.

3. Transfer the mixture to the prepared tin and bake in the middle of the oven for 55 minutes. To check if it is cooked, insert a piece of dry spaghetti into the middle of the cake; if it comes out clean and dry, it's ready. If not, cook it for a few more minutes.

4. Turn the sweet bread out onto a wire rack to cool and enjoy with your favourite cup of coffee.

Index

A

almonds: bitter chocolate and almond
squares 234
Amaretti and chocolate mousse
cake 232
Amaretto liqueur, chocolate panforte
with 237
anchovies, whole salmon with roasted
peppers, potatoes and 101
antipasti 14–39
aperitivi 14–39
Aperol Spritz 38
apples: apples poached in red wine
with Amaretti biscuit cream 240
classic Italian apple strudel 239
artichokes: artichoke and lemon soup
57
smoked trout with artichokes and
cannellini beans 29
the ultimate tomato, pepper,
artichoke and bread salad 204
asparagus: chicken in balsamic vinegar
with asparagus and cherry tomato
salad 158
baked rice with peas, pancetta and
asparagus 212
beans and asparagus salad with
balsamic glaze 215
aubergines: aubergine, tomato and
mozzarella stack 24
baked pasta with aubergines, red
onions and Parmesan 129
baked risotto with aubergine, basil
and mozzarella 138

B

bakes 60–79
balsamic vinegar: beans and asparagus
salad with balsamic glaze 215
roasted tomatoes with balsamic
vinegar 208
bananas: pear and banana sweet bread
248

basil: baked risotto with aubergine,
basil and mozzarella 139
basil sauce 92
creamy pesto dip 36
pasta with pesto, green beans and
potatoes 126
sardines with basil and lemon butter
26
beans: beans and asparagus salad with
balsamic glaze 215
Culatello, onion and bean soup 44
three-bean salad 168
see also cannellini beans
béchamel sauce 116
beef: beef and cannellini bean soup
48–9
Florentine pasta shells stuffed with
beef and béchamel sauce 116–17
marinated beef skewers with a three-
bean salad 168
Modena-style trio of meats with chilli
and rosemary 173
my grandfather's tagliatelle with
Bolognese sauce 112
pasta with sweet red onions, chilli
and fillet steak 124
biscotti: apples poached in red wine
with Amaretti biscuit cream 240
double chocolate, pistachio and chilli
biscotti 246
biscuits: Florentine biscuits 242
lady's kisses 245
Bologna-style rigatoni with mortadella
and chicken 109
Bolognese sauce 112
bread 180
Ligurian loaf with Taggiasca black
olives 193
pear and banana sweet bread 248
three cicchetti 16
traditional folded bread with
Genovese pesto 188–9
the ultimate tomato, pepper,
artichoke and bread salad 204
white fish soup with melted Taleggio
toasts 52–3

C

cabbage: Savoy cabbage with
pancetta and white wine 213
cakes: Amaretti and chocolate mousse
cake 232
polenta cake with oranges and
Cointreau 230
calf's liver: Venetian-style calf's liver in
white wine and sage sauce 161
cannellini beans: beef and cannellini
bean soup 48–9
pan-fried sea bass with cannellini
mash and basil sauce 92
smoked trout with artichokes and
cannellini beans 29
spicy cannellini bean and spinach
stew 78
capers: caper and butter sauce 102
carrots, griddled 102
casseroles: chicken and porcini
mushroom 73
slow-cooked veal 72
cheese: aubergine, tomato and
mozzarella stack 24
baked pasta with aubergines, red
onions and Parmesan 129
baked polenta with oozing
Gorgonzola 76–7
baked risotto with aubergine, basil
and mozzarella 139
creamy pesto dip 36
crispy chicken breast stuffed with
mozzarella and pesto 156
four-cheese risotto with fresh chives
142
Gorgonzola and prosciutto wraps
20–1
griddled courgette salad with chilli
dressing 30
traditional Italian rice salad 148
leek, Taleggio and pine kernel risotto
151
pasta with pesto, green beans and
potatoes 126
Piedmont pizza with Taleggio and
parsley 183
pizza filled with Taleggio and

rocket leaves 192

pizza with courgettes, chilli and fresh mint 184

potato and roasted pumpkin gnocchi 120

potato and smoked salmon crocchette 91

red pepper, Taleggio and courgette salad 206

red peppers stuffed with Taleggio 32–3

T-bone steak with courgette ribbons and goat's cheese 174

traditional folded bread with Genovese pesto 188–9

Treviso-style risotto with radicchio and dry vermouth 145

Tuscan baked fennel 74

white fish soup with melted Taleggio toasts 52–3

see also mascarpone cheese; ricotta cheese

chicken: Bologna-style rigatoni with mortadella and chicken 109

chicken and porcini mushroom casserole 73

chicken in balsamic vinegar with asparagus and cherry tomato salad 158

chicken in mascarpone sauce 69

crispy chicken baked with lemon and fennel 67

crispy chicken breast stuffed with mozzarella and pesto 156

simple Italian-style roast chicken with thyme and garlic 160

traditional north Italian chicken soup 46

chicken liver pâté with Marsala wine 18

chillies: chilli dressing 30

double chocolate, pistachio and chilli biscotti 246

Modena-style trio of meats with chilli and rosemary 173

octopus and potatoes with lemon and chilli 88–9

pasta with sweet red onions, chilli

and fillet steak 124

pizza with courgettes, chilli and fresh mint 184

prawn skewers with lemon, butter and chilli 23

spicy potato salad 198

chocolate: Amaretti and chocolate mousse cake 232

bitter chocolate and almond squares 234

chocolate ice cream with raisins and chocolate chips 227

chocolate panforte with Amaretto liqueur 237

coffee pots with melting chocolate 225

double chocolate, pistachio and chilli biscotti 246

Florentine biscuits 242

lady's kisses 245

ricotta mousse with chocolate and cinnamon sauce 224

sweet pasta filled with ricotta, hazelnuts, orange and chocolate 228

cicchetti: courgette 16

crispy cod 16

prawn 16

three cicchetti 16

clementines: Cantaloupe melon granita 222–3

cod: crispy cod cicchetti 16

fresh cod and red onion frittata 94

coffee pots with melting chocolate 225

Cointreau, polenta cake with oranges and 230

courgettes: courgette and ricotta tart 35

courgette cicchetti 16

griddled courgette salad with chilli dressing 30

pizza with courgettes, chilli and fresh mint 184

red pepper, Taleggio and courgette salad 206

T-bone steak with courgette ribbons and goat's cheese 174

crab: risotto with fresh crab, lemon and parsley 140

crocchette, potato and smoked salmon 91

Culatello, onion and bean soup 44

D

desserts 218–49

dip, creamy pesto 36

dressing, chilli 30

drinks: Aperol spritz 38

E

eggs: fresh cod and red onion frittata 94

F

fennel: crispy chicken baked with lemon and fennel 67

smooth fennel and tomato soup with prawns 50

Tuscan baked fennel 74

fettuccine: fresh Ligurian fettuccine 115

figs: baked figs with honey and vanilla mascarpone 220

Gorgonzola and prosciutto wraps 20–1

fish 82–103

white fish soup with melted Taleggio toasts 52–3

see cod; sea bass, etc

Florentine biscuits 242

Florentine pasta shells stuffed with beef and béchamel sauce 116–17

folded bread with Genovese pesto, traditional 188–9

frittata, fresh cod and red onion 94

G

game 154–76

garlic: crushed potatoes with garlic, sage and rosemary 201

sautéed potatoes with garlic and thyme 203

simple Italian-style roast chicken with thyme and garlic 160

Genovese pesto 188–9

ginger: Florentine biscuits 242

gnocchi, potato and roasted pumpkin 120

goat's cheese, T-bone steak with courgette ribbons and 174

granita, Cantaloupe melon 222–3

green beans: pasta with pesto, green beans and potatoes 126

spicy cannellini bean and spinach stew 78

grissini wrapped in Parma ham with a creamy pesto dip 36

H

ham: baby leeks with peas and crispy Parma ham 210

calzone with ricotta cheese and Parma ham 190–1

Gorgonzola and prosciutto wraps 20–1

grissini wrapped in Parma ham with a creamy pesto dip 36

roasted monkfish wrapped in Parma ham 97

veal shanks with Parma ham and white wine 165

hazelnuts: chocolate panforte with Amaretto liqueur 237

Florentine biscuits 242

sweet pasta filled with ricotta, hazelnuts, orange and chocolate 228

honey: baked figs with honey and vanilla mascarpone 220

honey ice cream 233

I

ice cream: chocolate ice cream with raisins and chocolate chips 227

honey ice cream 233

Italian apple strudel, classic 239

Italian rice salad, traditional 148

Italian-style roast chicken with thyme and garlic, simple 160

L

lady's kisses 245

lamb: lamb escalopes with wild mushrooms and white wine 176

proper northern Italian meatballs 171

stewed neck of lamb in thyme and red wine 70

langoustines, lemon-dressed raw 98

leeks: baby leeks with peas and crispy Parma ham 210

leek, Taleggio and pine kernel risotto 151

pappardelle with sausages and leeks 119

lemons: artichoke and lemon soup 57

baked citrus sea bass 63

crispy chicken baked with lemon and fennel 67

lemon-dressed raw langoustines 98

octopus and potatoes with lemon and chilli 88–9

prawn skewers with lemon, butter and chilli 23

risotto with fresh crab, lemon and parsley 140

sardines with basil and lemon butter 26

spinach and lemon soup 54

whole roasted sea bream with potatoes and samphire 64

Ligurian fettuccine 115

Ligurian loaf with Taggiasca black olives 193

linguine with mussels and black pepper 122

M

Marsala wine: chicken liver pâté with Marsala wine 18

mushroom soup with Marsala wine 56

mascarpone cheese: apples poached in red wine with Amaretti biscuit cream 240

baked figs with honey and vanilla mascarpone 220

chicken in mascarpone sauce 69

creamy pesto dip 36

roasted pheasant in red wine sauce 162

white pizza with potatoes, rosemary and mascarpone cheese 186

mayonnaise 16

meat 154–77

meatballs, proper northern Italian 171

melon: Cantaloupe melon granita 222–3

Modena-style trio of meats with chilli and rosemary 173

monkfish: roasted monkfish wrapped in Parma ham 97

mortadella: Bologna-style rigatoni with mortadella and chicken 109

mousse: Amaretti and chocolate mousse cake 232

ricotta mousse with chocolate and cinnamon sauce 224

mushrooms: chicken and porcini mushroom casserole 73

lamb escalopes with wild mushrooms and white wine 176

mushroom soup with Marsala wine 56

pappardelle with sausages and leeks 119

mussels: linguine with mussels and black pepper 122

seafood risotto 143

N

north Italian chicken soup, traditional 46

northern Italian meatballs, proper 171

O

octopus and potatoes with lemon and chilli 88–9

olives: Ligurian loaf with Taggiasca black olives 193

rabbit in white wine, rosemary, olive and tomato sauce 167

onions: baked pasta with aubergines, red onions and Parmesan 129

Culatello, onion and bean soup 44

fresh cod and red onion frittata 94

pasta with sweet red onions, chilli

and fillet steak 124
Tuscan-style roasted potatoes with red onions 200
oranges: baked citrus sea bass 63
polenta cake with oranges and Cointreau 230

P

pancetta: baked rice with peas, pancetta and asparagus 212
braised scallops with peas and sun-dried tomatoes 87
chicken in balsamic vinegar with asparagus and cherry tomato salad 158
Culatello, onion and bean soup 44
roasted pheasant in red wine sauce 162
Savoy cabbage with pancetta and white wine 213
traditional Venetian rice dish with pancetta and peas 147
panforte: chocolate panforte with Amaretto liqueur 237
pappardelle with sausages and leeks 119
Parma ham: baby leeks with peas and crispy Parma ham 210
calzone with ricotta cheese and Parma ham 190–1
Gorgonzola and prosciutto wraps 20–1
grissini wrapped in Parma ham with a creamy pesto dip 36
roasted monkfish wrapped in Parma ham 97
veal shanks with Parma ham and white wine 165
pasta 106–29
baked pasta with aubergines, red onions and Parmesan 129
Bologna-style rigatoni with mortadella and chicken 109
Florentine pasta shells stuffed with beef and béchamel sauce 116–17
fresh Ligurian fettuccine 115
linguine with mussels and black

pepper 122
my grandfather's tagliatelle with Bolognese sauce 112
pappardelle with sausages and leeks 119
pasta with pesto, green beans and potatoes 126
pasta with rabbit ragù 110
pasta with sweet red onions, chilli and fillet steak 124
spaghetti with king prawns and tuna 125
sweet pasta filled with ricotta, hazelnuts, orange and chocolate 228
pâté: chicken liver pâté with Marsala wine 18
pearl barley: beef and cannellini bean soup 48–9
pear and banana sweet bread 248
peas: baby leeks with peas and crispy Parma ham 210
baked rice with peas, pancetta and asparagus 212
braised scallops with peas and sun-dried tomatoes 87
traditional Venetian rice dish with pancetta and peas 147
pennette: pasta with sweet red onions, chilli and fillet steak 124
peppers: red pepper, Taleggio and courgette salad 206
red peppers stuffed with Taleggio 32–3
the ultimate tomato, pepper, artichoke and bread salad 204
whole salmon with roasted peppers, potatoes and anchovies 101
pesto: creamy pesto dip 36
crispy chicken breast stuffed with mozzarella and pesto 156
Genovese pesto 188–9
pasta with pesto, green beans and potatoes 126
pheasant: roasted pheasant in red wine sauce 162
Piedmont pizza with Taleggio and

parsley 183
pine kernels: leek, Taleggio and pine kernel risotto 151
pistachio nuts: double chocolate, pistachio and chilli biscotti 246
pizza 180
calzone with ricotta cheese and Parma ham 190–1
Piedmont pizza with Taleggio and parsley 183
pizza filled with Taleggio and rocket leaves 192
pizza with courgettes, chilli and fresh mint 184
white pizza with potatoes, rosemary and mascarpone cheese 186
polenta: baked polenta with oozing Gorgonzola 76–7
polenta cake with oranges and Cointreau 230
porcini mushrooms: chicken and porcini mushroom casserole 73
mushroom soup with Marsala wine 56
pappardelle with sausages and leeks 119
pork: Modena-style trio of meats with chilli and rosemary 173
my grandfather's tagliatelle with Bolognese sauce 112
proper northern Italian meatballs 171
potatoes: crushed potatoes with garlic, sage and rosemary 201
octopus and potatoes with lemon and chilli 88–9
pasta with pesto, green beans and potatoes 126
potato and roasted pumpkin gnocchi 120
potato and smoked salmon crocchette 91
sautéed potatoes with garlic and thyme 203
spicy potato salad 198
Tuscan-style roasted potatoes with red onions 200
white pizza with potatoes, rosemary

INDEX

and mascarpone cheese 186
whole roasted sea bream with
    potatoes and samphire 64
whole salmon with roasted peppers,
    potatoes and anchovies 101
prawns: prawn cicchetti 16
    prawn skewers with lemon, butter
        and chilli 23
    seafood risotto 143
    smooth fennel and tomato soup with
        prawns 50
    spaghetti with king prawns and tuna
        125
prosciutto: Gorgonzola and prosciutto
    wraps 20–1
Prosecco: Aperol Spritz 38
pumpkin: potato and roasted pumpkin
    gnocchi 120

R

rabbit: pasta with rabbit ragù 110
    rabbit in white wine, rosemary, olive
        and tomato sauce 167
radicchio: risotto with red radicchio
    and Italian sausages 137
    Treviso-style risotto with radicchio
        and dry vermouth 145
ragù, rabbit 110
raisins: chocolate ice cream with raisins
    and chocolate chips 227
rice 132–51
    baked rice with peas, pancetta and
        asparagus 212
    four-cheese risotto with fresh chives
        142
    leek, Taleggio and pine kernel risotto
        151
    risotto with fresh crab, lemon and
        parsley 140
    risotto with red radicchio and Italian
        sausages 137
    seafood risotto 143
    simple saffron risotto 134
    traditional Italian rice salad 148
    traditional Venetian rice dish with
        pancetta and peas 147
    Treviso-style risotto with radicchio

and dry vermouth 145
ricotta cheese: calzone with ricotta
    cheese and Parma ham 190–1
courgette and ricotta tart 35
ricotta mousse with chocolate and
    cinnamon sauce 224
pizza filled with Taleggio and
    rocket leaves 192
sweet pasta filled with ricotta,
    hazelnuts, orange and chocolate
    228
rigatoni: Bologna-style rigatoni with
    mortadella and chicken 109
risotto 132
    baked risotto with aubergine, basil
        and mozzarella 139
    four-cheese risotto with fresh chives
        142
    leek, Taleggio and pine kernel risotto
        151
    risotto with fresh crab, lemon and
        parsley 140
    risotto with red radicchio and Italian
        sausages 137
    seafood 143
    simple saffron 134
    Treviso-style risotto with radicchio
        and dry vermouth 145
rocket: Gorgonzola and prosciutto
    wraps 20–1
    pizza filled with Taleggio and
        rocket leaves 192
rosemary: crushed potatoes with
    garlic, sage and rosemary 201
    Modena-style trio of meats with chilli
        and rosemary 173
    rabbit in white wine, rosemary, olive
        and tomato sauce 167
    white pizza with potatoes, rosemary
        and mascarpone cheese 186

S

saffron: simple saffron risotto 134
sage: crushed potatoes with garlic,
    sage and rosemary 201
    white wine and sage sauce 161
salads 196–7

asparagus and cherry tomato 158
beans and asparagus salad with
    balsamic glaze 215
griddled courgette salad with chilli
    dressing 30
red pepper, Taleggio and courgette
    206
three-bean 168
traditional Italian rice 148
the ultimate tomato, pepper,
    artichoke and bread 204
salmon: potato and smoked salmon
    crocchette 91
    whole salmon with roasted peppers,
        potatoes and anchovies 101
samphire, whole roasted sea bream
    with potatoes and 64
sardines with basil and lemon butter 26
sauces: basil 92
    béchamel 116
    Bolognese 112
    caper and butter 102
    chocolate and cinnamon 224
    mascarpone 69
    red wine 162
    spicy tomato 84
    white wine and sage 161
    white wine, rosemary, olive and
        tomato 167
sausages: traditional Italian rice salad
    148
    Modena-style trio of meats with chilli
        and rosemary 173
    pappardelle with sausages and leeks
        119
    risotto with red radicchio and Italian
        sausages 137
Savoy cabbage with pancetta and
    white wine 213
scallops: braised scallops with peas
    and sun-dried tomatoes 87
    seafood risotto 143
sea bass: baked citrus sea bass 63
    pan-fried sea bass with cannellini
        mash and basil sauce 92
    sea bass with caper and butter
        sauce, with griddled carrots 102

sea bream: whole roasted sea bream with potatoes and samphire 64
seafood 82–3
  braised scallops with peas and sun-dried tomatoes 87
  lemon-dressed raw langoustines 98
  linguine with mussels and black pepper 122
  octopus and potatoes with lemon and chilli 88–9
  prawn cicchetti 16
  prawn skewers with lemon, butter and chilli 23
  risotto with fresh crab, lemon and parsley 140
  seafood risotto 143
  slow-cooked squid in a spicy tomato sauce 84
  smooth fennel and tomato soup with prawns 50
  spaghetti with king prawns and tuna 125
side dishes 196–7
skewers: marinated beef skewers with a three-bean salad 168
  prawn skewers with lemon, butter and chilli 23
smoked salmon, potato and smoked salmon crocchette 91
soups 42–57
  artichoke and lemon 57
  beef and cannellini bean 48–9
  Culatello, onion and bean 44
  mushroom soup with Marsala wine 56
  smooth fennel and tomato soup with prawns 50
  spinach and lemon 54
  traditional north Italian chicken 46
  white fish soup with melted Taleggio toasts 52–3
spaghetti with king prawns and tuna 125
spicy potato salad 198
spinach: spicy cannellini bean and spinach stew 78
  spinach and lemon soup 54

squid: slow-cooked squid in a spicy tomato sauce 84
stews 60
  spicy cannellini bean and spinach stew 78
  see also casseroles
strudel, classic Italian apple 239
sultanas: Florentine biscuits 242
sun-dried tomatoes, braised scallops with peas and 87

T
tagliatelle: my grandfather's tagliatelle with Bolognese sauce 112
tart, courgette and ricotta 35
thyme: sautéed potatoes with garlic and thyme 203
  simple Italian-style roast chicken with thyme and garlic 160
  stewed neck of lamb in thyme and red wine 70
tomatoes: asparagus and cherry tomato salad 158
  aubergine, tomato and mozzarella stack 24
  braised scallops with peas and sun-dried tomatoes 87
  rabbit in white wine, rosemary, olive and tomato sauce 167
  roasted tomatoes with balsamic vinegar 208
  slow-cooked squid in a spicy tomato sauce 84
  smooth fennel and tomato soup with prawns 50
  the ultimate tomato, pepper, artichoke and bread salad 204
tortiglioni: baked pasta with aubergines, red onions and Parmesan 129
Treviso-style risotto with radicchio and dry vermouth 145
trout: smoked trout with artichokes and cannellini beans 29
tuna: traditional Italian rice salad 148
  spaghetti with king prawns and tuna 125

turnips: traditional north Italian chicken soup 46
Tuscan baked fennel 74
Tuscan-style roasted potatoes with red onions 200

V
vanilla: baked figs with honey and vanilla mascarpone 220
veal: slow-cooked veal casserole 72
  veal shanks with Parma ham and white wine 165
Venetian rice dish with pancetta and peas, traditional 147
Venetian-style calf's liver in white wine and sage sauce 161
vermouth: Treviso-style risotto with radicchio and dry vermouth 145

W
wine: apples poached in red wine with Amaretti biscuit cream 240
  lamb escalopes with wild mushrooms and white wine 176
  rabbit in white wine, rosemary, olive and tomato sauce 167
  red wine, stewed neck of lamb in thyme and red wine 70
  roasted pheasant in red wine sauce 162
  Savoy cabbage with pancetta and white wine 213
  veal shanks with Parma ham and white wine 165
  white wine and sage sauce 161
wraps, Gorgonzola and prosciutto 20–1

INDEX

First published in Great Britain in 2014
by Hodder & Stoughton
An Hachette UK company

1

A CIP catalogue record for this title is available from the British Library.

Hardback ISBN 978 1 444 79738 1
Ebook ISBN 978 1 444 79739 8

Design by Georgia Vaux

Typeset in Gotham and Bodoni Black

Printed and bound in Germany by Mohn media

Hodder & Stoughton policy is to use papers that are natural, renewable and recyclable products and made from wood grown in sustainable forests. The logging and manufacturing processes are expected to conform to the environmental regulations of the country of origin.

Hodder & Stoughton Ltd
338 Euston Road
London NW1 3BH

www.hodder.co.uk

Acknowledgements:

A big thank you goes to my publisher and everyone at Hodder & Stoughton for allowing me once again to write a book with them. I had lots of fun and you guys are fantastic. To my wife and family for the continuous support and patience during my 'moody' writing days – you are always so good to me and I love you so much. Grazie to everyone at ITV for trusting me with the second series of Gino's Italian Escape. You are a bunch of crazy people – carry on being crazy please! A big kiss to Gee Charman and Matt Russell for always looking after me and making sure that the book – and especially the food – looks amazing. Thank you to Alison and Darren Shalson for making sure that all my recipes were checked and tasted before the final print. You guys were incredible and sorry for all the extra weight you put on! Big love to all the team at My Pasta Bar and Jeremy Hicks Associates, without your support it would have been impossible to write this book. As usual the BIGGEST THANK YOU goes to YOU, for continuing to buy my books and support my career. I LOVE YOU xxxx

Follow me on Facebook or on Twitter, @Ginofantastico